FAST AND HEALTHY
FAMILY COOKING

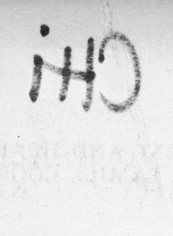

FAST AND HEALTHY
FAMILY COOKING

Beverley Piper

Thorsons
An Imprint of HarperCollins*Publishers*

For Malcolm

Thorsons
An Imprint of HarperCollins*Publishers*
77–85 Fulham Palace Road,
Hammersmith, London W6 8JB

Published by Thorsons 1993
10 9 8 7 6 5 4 3 2 1

© Beverley Piper 1993

Beverley Piper asserts the moral right to
be identified as the author of this work

A catalogue record for this book
is available from the British Library

ISBN 0 7225 2757 8

Typeset by Harper Phototypesetters Limited,
Northampton, England
Printed in Great Britain by
HarperCollinsManufacturing Glasgow

CONTENTS

ACKNOWLEDGEMENTS

TINA DORMAN
For her invaluable help, support and dedication, particularly in the Americanization of the book and the endless checking of the manuscript.

DEBORAH MILLER
Who, with professional expertise, assisted in testing the recipes and who helped me, as usual, with unflagging energy in preparing the recipes for the camera.

MALCOLM JARVIS AND ADAM PIPER
Without whom the book would never have become a reality. They helped in so many ways, lifting the shopping, tasting the recipes and boosting my morale when I thought I'd never meet the deadline!

TREVOR SUTTON
The photographer who took the photographs for this book at his large studio near my home, in Kent.

TIM AND PAM HUCKSTEPP
From the Pottery, Barrow Hill, Sellinge, Ashford, Kent, for so kindly loaning me some of their extensive range of hand-thrown pots to use in the photographs.

INTRODUCTION

If you are out at work all day, a parent with young children, a retired person busy with hobbies or grandchildren, or perhaps a student studying for examinations, I'm sure you don't have time to spend hours ploughing through complicated recipes when you need to eat fast.

The recipes in this book fall into three categories – vegan, vegetarian and demi-veg, which means with chicken and fish, and they cater for people like you who don't have much spare time but who want to eat healthily and who enjoy and take an interest in the food they prepare.

Healthy eating means cutting down on fat, particularly saturated fat, eating more fibre and less salt and sugar, and eating more fruit and vegetables. For optimum health we need to combine all these things and provide for ourselves, our families and friends, an interesting, varied and well-balanced diet.

The recipes in this book are all fairly short, so the lists of ingredients are uncomplicated. Most of the recipes use ordinary foods which you will probably have in the fridge, freezer or store cupboard anyway – try to keep the foods listed on pages 12–15 constantly in stock; that way you'll find it particularly quick and easy to put the recipes together, and your eating habits will change naturally by replacing less healthy meals with these healthy, filling alternatives.

I found that the easiest way to change the bad eating habits of my family was simply to stop buying the less healthy foods, but I must admit it was a very gradual process; being too rigid about it is a surefire way to put everyone off!

To make a start, try switching to wholewheat bread. Buy

it in bulk at the supermarket and freeze it. Everyone loves toast, and sliced wholewheat bread toasts well straight from the freezer.

For spreading use low-fat polyunsaturated spreads. Luckily my family loves Bovril and Marmite (beef-extract and yeast-extract spreads), both of which have valuable amounts of vitamin B, but we also use peanut butter, honey, marmalade and occasionally reduced-sugar jams (jelly) – they're so fruity!

Try to follow a somewhat 'peasant'-style diet and eat lots of unrefined foods. Homemade soups are a great favourite in our household – I often simmer root vegetables in stock, with fresh herbs, then blend the contents of the pan to a purée for a filling, wholesome lunch, or I add a can of drained beans to the soup and don't bother to blend – you'll find plenty of tasty soup recipes in this book.

Pasta is another great favourite with us, including Oriental-style noodles, which are extremely quick to cook. Try a steaming plateful of nutty-tasting wholegrain noodles, cooked in a trice, topped with a tasty vegetable stir fry – so quick to put together, and healthy and popular too; teenagers especially seem to love pasta.

Often someone in the family is trying to lose weight and I have found that a plateful of mixed vegetables or a large salad served with pulses (legumes) and a low-fat dressing, plus a garnish of protein – cheese, eggs, nuts, seeds, chopped skinned chicken or lightly cooked or canned fish, makes a visually attractive meal that is filling and well liked. If you add a can of pulses (legumes) or a portion of cooked pasta the meal is more filling, so there is less temptation to eat too much of the cheese, meat etc.

Warm, crusty wholewheat bread reheated in the oven makes a wonderful meal accompaniment that's pretty instant, and the appetizing aroma it produces wafts through the house quickly too! People really will be too full after a healthy, well-balanced main course to indulge in sticky puddings or chocolate.

Why we should eat more healthily

In 1991 the World Health Organization told us in no uncertain terms that for the sake of our health we must change to a more Mediterranean-style diet. This means eating more fibre, less fat, particularly saturated fat, and less salt and sugar. This recommendation followed the discovery that natives of Mediterranean countries suffer far fewer diet-related diseases such as heart-attacks, strokes, diabetes etc. and have a lower rate of cancer.

Cooking methods

The way food is cooked has a direct effect on the nutrients it contains. To preserve the nutrients as much as possible, always choose grilling (broiling), poaching, microwaving or stir frying, using the minimum of added fat when absolutely necessary. If you do use fat ensure that it's polyunsaturated – the label will tell you whether it's saturated or polyunsaturated. Hard fats such as lard, butter and hard margarines are all saturated. Some of the recipes in this book use a little butter for its superior flavour, but do keep it as an occasional treat rather than an everyday part of your diet.

Baking

Don't feel that eating healthily means you can no longer enjoy home baking. Just switch to wholewheat flour instead of refined white and cut down on sugar, using raw cane sugar or honey when you need a little sweetness. Try the Carrot Cake (page 172) or the Apple Sponge (page 164) – both use healthy ingredients to produce absolutely delicious family bakes. Sadly the Carrot Cake never lasts more than a day in my house, but it does freeze well without the topping, so I nearly always bake two in order to have one ready if people arrive unexpectedly for tea – it defrosts rapidly in the microwave.

FOODS FOR THOUGHT

A few words about how to eat more healthily with some of the foods used in this book.

Fats

A certain amount of dietary fat is useful as a source of energy but too much saturated fat has been linked to illnesses such as heart disease, diabetes and certain types of cancer. Fat is found in varying amounts in just about every food we eat, so it is a good idea to cut down on added fat. There are different kinds of fat and it does help to understand a little about this food and therefore appreciate why most of the fats used in this book are polyunsaturated.

All fat is high in calories: one gram contains nine kilocalories, while one gram of protein or carbohydrate contains only four kilocalories. Hard fats, mostly derived from animals, butter, lard and hard margarines, have been associated with heart disease, as they tend to clog up the arteries with fatty deposits, making it more difficult for the blood to flow through easily.

Liquid fats such as polyunsaturated oils and soft polyunsaturated margarines are mostly derived from vegetable sources and should be used whenever possible in cooking and spreading, since it is now thought that polyunsaturates help prevent the arteries clogging up. Check the label of the oil or margarine you buy to find out if it is polyunsaturated. Olive oils are high in monounsaturates and antioxidants which are also now thought to help reduce blood cholesterol levels and to assist the blood in flowing easily.

Cholesterol is a particular type of fat that ends up in the walls of our arteries, often causing heart problems. It is essential to the human body but only in very small amounts, and since the body produces all the cholesterol it needs on its own it can be dangerous to take in extra by frequently eating high-cholesterol foods. These include egg yolks, liver and kidneys, and to a lesser extent, some shellfish such as prawns (shrimps) and lobster, so these foods should be eaten in moderation. Where eggs are used in the recipes in this book, quantities have been calculated according to UK standard size 3 (medium-sized).

100% wholewheat flour

Wholewheat flour, also known as wholemeal flour, is, as the name suggests, whole flour, containing the valuable outer husk (bran) and wheatgerm as well as protein and starch, with vitamins and minerals.

Wholewheat flour is used throughout the recipes in this book and is readily available in supermarkets in both plain and self-raising (self-rising) varieties. Ensure you always have a supply of each in the cupboard; it is exceptionally good in baking, has a delicious nutty flavour and is also wonderful for thickening soups and stews etc., when it can either be blended with a little cold water and stirred in, or simply sprinkled on to the ingredients then whisked or stirred in.

Wholewheat pasta

Higher in fibre and protein than its white counterpart, wholewheat pasta takes a little longer to cook but it tastes far better and is more filling. It is available in a variety of shapes, including spaghetti – serve it with low-fat sauces. Try Pasta with Corn and Tomatoes on page 41 or Golden Pasta Bake on page 136.

Oats

Oats, commonly purchased as rolled oats, contain some protein, are a valuable carbohydrate food and a useful ingredient in healthy cookery. They can be used in sweet and savoury dishes and are particularly good in baking. They are very popular now in muesli but don't make the mistake of combining oats with too much sugar or fat – remember porridge is delicious made with half water and half low-fat milk, served with 2 teaspoons clear honey and a little cinnamon per portion, but not so healthy with golden syrup and cream!

Rice

This valuable cereal is cultivated in hot countries such as India, Java, China and Japan. It is the staple food of over half the human race.

Brown or unpolished rice retains valuable vitamins, particularly the B group of vitamins and has a delicious nutty flavour. It does take a little longer to cook than white rice, which has had the outer husk removed, but it is a valuable carbohydrate and an extremely versatile, energy-giving food.

For the majority of recipes in this book I have used easy-cook brown rice, which contains all the goodness of brown rice but has been treated so it cooks more quickly. Try keeping cooked, drained rice covered in the refrigerator for up to 5 days. Use it as an invaluable standby for quick meals as it re-heats quickly.

Gelozone (setting powder)

This is an excellent vegetarian alternative to gelatine; it produces an almost clear transparent jelly and is very easy to use. One teaspoon will set 1 pint (600ml/2½ cups) of liquid.

Gelozone is derived from Irish moss and carrageen moss and is available in the UK in packets from healthfood stores; the American equivalent would be Kuzu. Types of seaweed can also be used in the same way – agar agar is a good example – so check with your healthfood store for advice.

It can be used to thicken soups and sauces and to set jellies (moulded desserts). Try Fruit Juice Set Dessert with Fresh Fruits on page 122.

Carob

Carob is the healthy alternative to cocoa, and since one in ten people are allergic to chocolate, it does make sense to switch to carob.

Carob is free from caffeine and theobromine. It is higher in natural sugar, fibre and iron than cocoa and lower in calories, fat and sodium.

Carob is available in powder form – use the same proportions as you would cocoa. It is also readily available in bars from healthfood shops.

Beans, peas and lentils

Beans, peas and lentils, known collectively as pulses or legumes, are the dried seeds of plants. They are high in fibre, a valuable source of protein and carbohydrate and also contain some B vitamins.

Dried beans and peas such as red kidney beans, chick peas, flageolet beans, black-eyed beans etc., need to be soaked in plenty of cold water for 8–12 hours before being drained and cooked in fresh water for 2–3 hours. Red and green lentils and split peas, however, may be cooked without soaking and are therefore particularly valuable to the cook in a hurry.

Fortunately canned cooked beans, peas and lentils are now available in supermarkets. These are a boon to the healthy eater as they may be drained, rinsed and used in salads or a variety of hot dishes.

Seeds

Seeds such as sunflower, caraway and sesame are valuable for their fat, which is high in polyunsaturates and low in saturates, and protein, and some are particularly rich in vitamin B. They add a delicious 'crunch' to both sweet and savoury recipes and are a versatile ingredient that needs no preparation.

Nuts

Although nuts are not usually eaten in sufficient quantities to play a particularly important part in the diet, they are important to vegetarians as they contain a valuable amount of protein. The fat content is also considerable so they should be used sparingly.

Nuts are a versatile ingredient; they may be chopped and added to cakes, biscuits and salads, sprinkled on top of dishes, both sweet and savoury, used ground or toasted and served on stir-fry dishes as a garnish. Keep almonds, cashew nuts, walnuts, pecan nuts, peanuts.

Sugar

Refined sugar is derived from sugar cane or beet. It is high in calories yet has no nutritional value, and nowadays, it is often eaten in such large quantities that it tends to lead to obesity. It can also cause tooth decay. Where a recipe does call for sugar, always use raw cane sugar which is dark brown in colour, has a good flavour and at least contains some minerals.

Honey

Bees make honey from nectar of blossoms as a food store for the winter months. It never goes off – a jar of Ancient Egyptian honey was found in a tomb at the beginning of this century and although the honey had discoloured it still tasted and smelt fresh!

Whether honey is clear or set depends on the balance of unrefined sugars. Clear, or runny, honey is particularly useful in cooking and can be used in place of sugar in many recipes. Remember, however, that honey is high in calories, containing approximately 85 calories per tablespoon.

Dried Fruits

Dried fruits include currants, sultanas (golden seedless raisins), raisins, dates, prunes, apricots, figs, pears and apples. They are a good source of natural sugar (carbohydrate) in the form of fructose, fibre and a variety of minerals. Apricots and prunes contribute a fair amount of vitamin A.

Nowadays dried fruits may be used straight from the packet, without washing. They are excellent in cakes and biscuits and in savoury dishes, particularly Indian ones such as curries and pilaffs. Dried fruit salad makes an excellent quick dessert, particularly if you use the no-need-to-soak varieties – serve with plain yoghurt or low-fat fromage frais.

Dairy Products

Low-fat alternatives to most dairy products are easily available nowadays. Use low-fat milk, which contains all the calcium but half the fat of full cream milk. Reduced-fat Cheddar cheese is sold in most supermarkets, and you could also try one of the new Cheddar-type cheeses made from polyunsaturated fat. Edam, Camembert, cottage and curd cheeses are all relatively low in fat, but as a general rule you should reduce your overall consumption of cheese.

Avoid cream, which is full of saturated fat. Single (light) cream has a minimum fat content of 18% so may be used as a luxury now and again. Whipping cream has a minimum fat content of 35% and double (heavy) cream 48%, whilst clotted cream has a rather frightening fat content of 55%. Soured cream, which is single (light) cream with the addition of a culture giving it a piquant refreshing taste and thicker consistency, has a fat content similar to single (light) cream – about 18%. You may prefer to use low-fat yoghurt, or fromage frais as a healthy alternative to cream.

Butter is made from the fat of milk by churning cream at a certain temperature. Although it has a wonderful flavour, it really is best avoided. Use polyunsaturated spreads and margarines, choosing reduced-fat alternatives where appropriate. Look out for the reduced-fat blends of whey and vegetable oils, which look like hard block margarine and have been specifically developed for cooking. They contain roughly 40% less saturated fat than traditional packet margarines and 25% less total fat and calories. They are suitable for all cooking purposes except deep-fat frying.

Tofu (soya [soy] bean curd)

Tofu is made from the soya (soy) bean. It is a versatile, high-protein food which has been used widely in Oriental countries for centuries.

Tofu is available in blocks and may be bought from the chilled counter of the healthfood store. It is a useful ingredient for vegetarians and may be added to stir fries, grilled (broiled) in kebabs, used to stuff vegetables, served with rice or added to salads. It may also be blended in the food processor and used to make cheesecakes and other desserts.

Vegetable Protein

Vegetable protein is another food which makes a versatile alternative to meat. It is full of dietary fibre with a very low fat content and no cholesterol. An excellent example is Quorn, which is harvested from a tiny plant, a relative of the mushroom. With only 85 kcalories per 100g, Quorn is a valuable addition to your diet. Quorn and other similar products are available from larger supermarkets and are already cooked, so only need reheating for as little as 4–5 minutes in a stir fry or sauté recipe or for up to 15 minutes in sauces and casseroles, to allow the flavours to develop.

As egg white may be used in the production of Quorn and other vegetable proteins, they are not suitable for vegans.

Fruit and vegetables

There are so many varieties of fruits and vegetables now available and so many different exciting ways of serving them, that eating more of them is one of the easiest ways to improve the quality of your diet.

Fruit and vegetables are a good source of fibre, vitamins and anti-oxidants. Anti-oxidants are natural substances that actually clothe the fat in the body during the digestive process, preventing it from furring up the arteries. Fibre-rich vegetables are low in calories and fill you up, so they have a valuable role to play for dieters and for everyone who prefers not to increase their waist line.

For best results eat fruit and vegetables raw as often as possible. If you do cook vegetables, steam, poach or microwave them in the minimum of liquid until just tender. Reserve the liquid the vegetables were cooked in to make a soup. Make sure your vegetables are as fresh as possible, as valuable vitamin C is rapidly lost on storage.

Salt

Cutting down on salt intake is a vital public health objective, stated the *British Medical Journal* in autumn 1991. If the average daily consumption per person could be reduced by two thirds it could save one person in five from a stroke and one person in six from heart disease – pretty alarming statistics.

There seems absolutely no doubt that a high intake of salt is a contributory cause of heart disease.

Salt is present in almost every manufactured food we buy, so the biggest impact would be achieved by persuading manufacturers to limit the amount of salt they add to processed foods. However we can do our bit in the home. The recipes in this book that include salt suggest 'a little sea salt', and that is exactly what should be used. Where salt is not listed, be brave and leave it out – you will find that food actually tastes better without it, as the natural flavours come through.

Lemon juice, herbs, tomatoes, garlic, etc. are all natural flavour enhancers which can be used in place of salt. Spices, particularly freshly ground black pepper, are useful too.

Never add salt when you cook vegetables – it tends to toughen them, so they take longer to cook – and lose the salt cellar so that the family can't add salt to their food at the table; it's only a habit that they're better without.

STOCKING UP

It is beneficial to have mainly 'healthy' ingredients in stock so I have listed staple foods that should start to feature in your various storage areas. Gradually ensure that these replace their unhealthy counterparts, and stop buying commercially prepared cakes, biscuits, pies etc. straight away. When the family demands a sweet snack, offer them a homebaked goodie which you know contains polyunsaturated fat, little sugar and plenty of fibre, such as the Carrot Cake on page 172 or the Apricot Slices on page 174. Try to buy fresh foods cheaply, when in season – make good use of local markets. Stock up on pulse vegetables which are cheaper than meat and better for you, and try to avoid expensive convenience foods which may be high in salt and fat.

Refrigerator

Low-fat polyunsaturated
  spreads
Reduced-fat
  polyunsaturated
  margarines suitable for
  baking
Eggs
Fresh fruit juice
Reduced-fat Cheddar cheese
Cottage cheese
Curd cheese
Edam cheese
Low-fat milk (soy)
Selection of salad leaves
Tomatoes
Mushrooms
Tofu
Vegetable protein (e.g.
  Quorn)
Plain low-fat yoghurt
Fromage frais ?
Lemons
Tomato juice
Celery
Selection of fresh herbs
Fresh chicken / seafood
Cooked long grain brown
  rice

Freezer

Wholewheat bread and rolls

Selection of white and oily
  fish plus frozen prawns
  (shrimps)
Chicken, whole and in
  portions
Selection of vegetables,
  particularly broccoli,
  beans, peas, sweetcorn
  (corn), spinach, mixed
  vegetables
Selection of fruit,
  particularly raspberries,
  redcurrants and
  blackcurrants
Reduced-fat shortcrust
  pastry

Store Cupboard

Dried pulses (legumes),
  particularly red and
  green lentils
Rolled oats
100% wholewheat plain
  and self-raising (self-
  rising) flour (multi-grain)
Arrowroot ?
Vegetable-based setting (asian market)
  powder (e.g. Gelozone)
Cans of reduced-fat
  evaporated milk
Cans of beans such as
  butter (lima) beans,

chick peas, red kidney
  beans, black-eyed beans
Brown rice (the easy-cook
  variety)
Wholewheat pasta
Pasta shapes and noodles
Cans of fruit in natural
  juice such as pineapple,
  apricots, blackcurrants
Carob powder and bars
Dried fruits such as
  apricots, raisins, sultanas
  (golden seedless raisins),
  prunes, currants
Honey, set for spreading
  and clear for cooking
Soy sauce
Worcestershire sauce
Selection of dried herbs
Raw cane sugar
Dried skimmed milk
Vegetable stock cubes
Selection of spices
High-fibre breakfast cereals
  without added sugar
Cans of fish in brine, water
  or polyunsaturated oil,
  such as salmon, tuna,
  sardines

*Fresh vegetables to buy
regularly, when in season*

Aubergines (eggplant)

Avocado pears
Brussels sprouts
Cabbage
Carrots
Cauliflower
Celery
Courgettes (zucchini)
Cucumber
Leeks
Mushrooms
Onions
Parsnips
Peas
Red and green (bell)
  peppers
Spinach
Swede (rutabaga)
Tomatoes
Watercress

*Fresh fruits to buy regularly,
when in season*

Apples
Bananas
Grapefruit
Grapes
Lemons
Mangoes
Melon
Nectarines
Oranges
Peaches

Pears
Pineapple
Plums
Raspberries

Rhubarb
Strawberries
Tangerines

HINTS FOR HEALTHY, SPEEDY FOOD

1. Don't peel fruits and vegetables unless absolutely necessary – they're quicker to use that way, and contain more nutrients too – but scrub clean under running water.
2. Grill, steam or bake foods for healthy eating, or stir fry quickly in the minimum of polyunsaturated oil.
3. Avoid hidden fats in foods such as cakes, biscuits, pies, pastries, mayonnaise and salad dressings.
4. Choose low-fat polyunsaturated spreads instead of butter for your morning toast and lunchtime sandwiches.
5. Switch to wholewheat bread for its high fibre content and valuable vitamin B group contribution to the diet.
6. Change from whole milk to low-fat to reduce fat consumption without losing valuable protein, calcium and vitamins.
7. Eat more complex carbohydrate foods such as wholewheat bread, potatoes, wholewheat pasta, wholegrain cereals and pulses (legumes). They really do fill you up and give you energy for long periods as well as providing fibre and other nutrients such as protein, minerals and vitamins.
8. Eat more fresh fruit and vegetables – for speed eat both raw. Most vegetables are delicious raw, particularly combined with a low-fat dressing enhanced with lemon juice and herbs.
9. Too much sodium (salt is 40 per cent sodium) may contribute towards high blood pressure, which can in turn increase the risk of developing coronary heart disease, strokes and kidney disease, so decrease the amount of salt you add to food; your taste buds will

quickly adjust as the natural flavour of the food starts to come through.

10. Use other flavourings instead of salt:
    Fresh herbs, such as mint, parsley, sage, thyme, etc.
    Lemon and lime juice, cider vinegar and wine vinegar
    Nutmeg, cinnamon and ginger
    Garlic, onion, and (bell) peppers
    Freshly ground black pepper, seeds such as sesame and poppy

11. Use plain yoghurt or fromage frais instead of cream in desserts such as mousses and cold soufflés.

Note: British standard measuring spoons have been used throughout the recipes, and the American equivalents are as follows:

British	American
1 teaspoon	1¼ teaspoonful
1 tablespoonful	1¼ tablespoonful

It is very important to follow *either* Imperial *or* Metric *or* American measurements within any recipe.

A microwave oven with an electrical output of 700w was used throughout.

SPEEDY SNACKS, STARTERS AND SOUPS

So often a tasty snack or a wholesome bowl of homemade soup with bread is all that's required when people want speedy food. Use starters together – two or three will make a delicious meal and are ideal for low-key entertaining, where guests help themselves from a selection of dishes.

Pink Salmon and Mushroom Pâté

Pink salmon provides protein and polyunsaturated fat as well as vitamins and calcium for healthy bones and teeth. The combination of mushrooms with salmon and dry Vermouth is delicious. Serve this pâté as a starter at your next dinner party or with chunks of fresh bread as a special snack.

PREPARATION TIME: *15 mins*   FREEZING: *Suitable at end of stage 4*
COOKING TIME: —   SERVES: *4*

Imperial (Metric)	*American*
15-ounce (425g) can pink salmon, drained	15-ounce can pink salmon, drained
1 oz (25g) butter	2 tablespoons butter
3 oz (75g) button mushrooms, sliced	¼ cup sliced button mushrooms
2 cloves garlic	2 cloves garlic
½ teaspoon ground dried bay leaves	½ teaspoon dried ground bay leaves
Freshly ground black pepper	Freshly ground black pepper
1–2 tablespoons dry Vermouth	1–2 tablespoons dry Vermouth

To garnish
1 button mushroom, sliced

1 Turn the salmon into a food processor, discarding the skin and bones.
2 Heat the butter in a medium pan, add the mushrooms and sauté for 2–3 minutes to soften slightly. Add the mushrooms to the processor with the pan juices.
3 Chop the garlic and add to the processor with the ground bay leaves. Season with the black pepper. Add the Vermouth.
4 Blend until smooth. Transfer to a pâté dish. Refrigerate for at least 30 minutes.
5 Serve decorated with the sliced mushroom.

Sunshine Soup

A filling winter-vegetable soup that tastes of summer!
Plenty of fibre and carbohydrate in this well-flavoured
soup, plus vitamin A. Serve with warm, crusty
poppyseed rolls before Florida Cocktail (page 36) for a
quick and easy lunch for guests.

PREPARATION TIME: *12 mins*   FREEZING: *Suitable at end of stage 7*
COOKING TIME: *25 mins*   SERVES: *4*

Imperial (Metric)	American
4 medium carrots	4 medium carrots
2 medium parsnips	2 medium parsnips
1 small onion	1 small onion
1 medium potato	1 medium potato
2 tablespoons sunflower oil	2 tablespoons sunflower oil
1 teaspoon dried thyme	1 teaspoon dried thyme
1 clove garlic, crushed	1 clove garlic, crushed
2 pints (1.2 litres) vegetable stock	5 cups vegetable stock
A little freshly ground black pepper	A little freshly ground black pepper

To garnish
Freshly chopped parsley

1 Dice the carrots, parsnips, and onion. Peel and chop the potato.
2 Heat the oil in a large pan, then sauté the onion with the carrots and parsnips for 5 minutes.
3 Add the potato to the pan and continue to sauté for a further 2–3 minutes.
4 Add the thyme and garlic to the vegetables, then pour over the stock and season with black pepper.
5 Bring to the boil, cover and simmer for 20–25 minutes, or until the vegetables are tender.
6 Blend the soup in a food processor in two batches. Return to the pan.
7 Reheat, stirring, until just below boiling point. Cool and freeze at this point if required.
8 Serve immediately sprinkled with the freshly chopped parsley.

Quick Pizzas

Italian pizzas are very popular but can be time consuming to prepare and bake. Try this speedy version made on large granary rolls. High in fibre and low in fat, these pizzas make a tasty snack at almost any time.

PREPARATION TIME: *10 mins*   FREEZING: *Suitable at end of stage 4*
COOKING TIME: *5–10 mins*   MAKES: *8 pizzas*

Imperial (Metric)	*American*
4 large granary bread rolls	4 large granary bread rolls
4 tomatoes	4 tomatoes
Freshly ground black pepper	Freshly ground black pepper
5 oz (150g) Mozzarella cheese	1 cup Mozzarella cheese
2 oz (50g) can anchovy fillets, drained	2-ounce can anchovy fillets, drained
A few pimento-stuffed olives, sliced	A few pimento-stuffed olives, sliced
1 teaspoon dried oregano	1 teaspoon dried oregano
2 tablespoons olive oil	2 tablespoons olive oil

1 Slice each bread roll in half horizontally and lightly toast on both sides.
2 Thinly slice the tomatoes and arrange them evenly over the baps. Season with black pepper.
3 Slice the cheese thinly and divide between the baps. Decorate with the drained anchovies and sliced olives.
4 Sprinkle with the oregano then drizzle the oil evenly over.
5 Grill (broil) until the cheese is melted and bubbling. Serve immediately.

Anchovy-Stuffed Eggs

Tasty, high in protein and filling, these attractive stuffed eggs can be served as a starter, high tea or light supper dish. French bread and a mixed salad will make them into a complete meal.

PREPARATION TIME: *15 mins*   FREEZING: *Not suitable*
COOKING TIME: *10 mins*   SERVES: *4*

Imperial (Metric)	*American*
4 eggs, hardboiled and shelled	4 eggs, hardcooked and shelled
2 oz (50g) low-fat spread	4 tablespoons low-fat spread
2 teaspoons anchovy essence	2 teaspoons anchovy essence
2 tablespoons reduced-calorie mayonnaise	2 tablespoons reduced calorie mayonnaise
Freshly ground black pepper	Freshly ground black pepper

To garnish
Fresh parsley
A selection of salad leaves

1 Cut each egg in half lengthwise.
2 Using a teaspoon, carefully remove the yolks and put them into a food processor. Blend to chop finely.
3 Add the low-fat spread, anchovy essence, mayonnaise and a seasoning of black pepper. Blend until quite smooth. It may be necessary to stop the machine and scrape the ingredients from the sides with a spatula, then process again.
4 Pipe or spoon the mixture into the egg white hollows.
5 To serve, arrange the eggs on the salad leaves and garnish each one with a sprig of parsley.

Celery and Herb Bread

Although this loaf takes about an hour to bake, it is particularly quick and easy to prepare, and you could use the time it takes to cook to make soup or a salad to serve with it. Plenty of protein, fibre and vitamin B in this savoury loaf, which is delicious sliced and served on its own or with low-fat spread at lunch or tea time. Also good toasted.

PREPARATION TIME: *15 mins* FREEZING: *Suitable*
COOKING TIME: *55 mins* MAKES: *1 lb (450g) loaf*

Imperial (Metric)	American
1 lb (450g) self raising wholemeal flour	3 cups self-rising wholewheat flour
1 teaspoon dried oregano	1 teaspoon dried oregano
1 clove garlic, crushed	1 clove garlic, crushed
4 oz (100g) reduced-fat Cheddar cheese, grated	1 cup grated reduced-fat Cheddar cheese
2 celery stalks	2 celery stalks
2 eggs	2 eggs
8 fl oz (250ml) water	1 cup water
2 tablespoons corn oil	2 tablespoons corn oil
A little sea salt and freshly ground black pepper	A little sea salt and freshly ground black pepper

1 Preheat the oven to gas mark 5, 375°F (190°C).
2 Lightly grease a 1 lb (450g) loaf tin.
3 Put the flour into a large mixing bowl. Add the oregano, garlic and half the grated cheese. Finely chop the celery and add to the bowl. Mix well.
4 Beat together the eggs, water and oil. Season lightly. Add to the dry ingredients and mix well.
5 Turn the mixture into the prepared tin. It will come right to the top. Sprinkle over the remaining cheese.
6 Stand the tin on a baking sheet and bake for approximately 55 minutes. Turn out on to a wire rack and allow to cool. Serve warm or cold, in thick slices.

Easy Cheesey Tomatoes

Tomatoes are a useful source of vitamins A and C and also provide some fibre, especially if the skins are eaten. They taste wonderful with this low-fat cheese and prawn (shrimp) filling. Serve as a healthy snack or a dinner-party starter with Melba toast or wholewheat bread.

PREPARATION TIME: *15 mins*   FREEZING: *Not suitable*
COOKING TIME: *20 mins*   SERVES: *4*

Imperial (Metric)	*American*
4 large tomatoes	4 large tomatoes
4 oz (100g) cottage cheese with chives	½ cup cottage cheese with chives
1 oz (25g) wholewheat breadcrumbs	2 tablespoons wholewheat breadcrumbs
3 oz (75g) peeled prawns, chopped	¼ cup chopped peeled shrimps
Freshly ground black pepper	Freshly ground black pepper
1 oz (25g) reduced-fat mature Cheddar cheese, grated	¼ cup grated reduced-fat mature Cheddar cheese

1 Preheat the oven to gas mark 4, 350°F (180°C). Cut ½ in (1 cm) off the top of each tomato. Scoop out the seeds and pass through a sieve, reserving juice.
2 Put the cottage cheese, breadcrumbs and prawns (shrimps) into a mixing bowl. Season with a little black pepper. Add 2 tablespoons juice reserved from the tomatoes. Mix well to combine.
3 Divide the filling between the tomatoes and arrange them on a baking sheet.
4 Sprinkle the Cheddar cheese on top of each stuffed tomato.
5 Bake for 15–20 minutes, until golden. Serve immediately.

Tomato and Apple Soup

This light, nourishing soup has a wonderful fresh flavour due to the combination of Bramley apple (or any cooking apple) and tomato juice. Serve it with warm wholewheat bread or homemade scones.

PREPARATION TIME: *15 mins*   FREEZING: *Suitable at end of stage 5*
COOKING TIME: *25 mins*   SERVES: *6*

Imperial (Metric)	American
1 medium carrot	1 medium carrot
1 medium onion	1 medium onion
1 medium cooking apple	1 medium baking apple
1 tablespoon sunflower oil	1 tablespoon sunflower oil
2 cloves garlic, crushed	2 cloves garlic, crushed
15 fl oz (450ml) tomato juice	2 cups tomato juice
1½ pints (900ml) vegetable stock	3¼ cups vegetable stock
1 teaspoon dried basil	1 teaspoon dried basil
A little sea salt and freshly ground black pepper	A little sea salt and freshly ground black pepper
6 tablespoons cooked brown rice	6 tablespoons cooked brown rice

1 Dice the carrot and onion. Core and roughly chop the apple.
2 Heat the oil in a large saucepan and sauté the vegetables and apple for 5 minutes, until the onion softens. Add the garlic and cook, stirring, for 2 minutes.
3 Add the tomato juice, stock, basil and seasoning. Bring to the boil, cover and simmer for 20 minutes.
4 Using a draining spoon, transfer the vegetables and apple to a food processor, add about 5 fl oz (150ml/⅔ cup) of the soup liquid and blend until smooth.
5 Return the purée to the liquid remaining in the pan.
6 Add the rice and stir well. Reheat and serve immediately.

Avocados with Light Herb Cheese

Ripe avocados filled with low-fat herby cheese and garnished with pecan nuts make a deliciously different starter that is particularly quick to prepare at the last minute. Serve with wholewheat bread. Avocados are quite high in fat, but it is monounsaturated, the type doctors recommend for a healthy heart. They are also rich in vitamins A, B, C, D, E and calcium.

PREPARATION TIME: *10 mins*   FREEZING: *Not suitable*
COOKING TIME: *15 mins chill time*   SERVES: *4*

Imperial (Metric)	American
6 oz (175g) curd cheese	1½ cups pot cheese
1 clove garlic, crushed	1 clove garlic, crushed
2 tablespoons fromage frais	2 tablespoons fromage frais
1–2 tablespoons pure orange juice	1–2 tablespoons pure orange juice
A little sea salt and freshly ground black pepper	A little sea salt and freshly ground black pepper
1 tablespoon freshly chopped chives	1 tablespoon freshly chopped chives
1 tablespoon freshly chopped basil	1 tablespoon freshly chopped basil
2 ripe avocados	2 ripe avocados
3 oz (75g) pecan nuts, chopped	⅔ cup chopped pecan nuts

1 Put the curd (pot) cheese into a mixing bowl. Add the garlic, fromage frais, orange juice and a seasoning of salt and pepper.
2 Mix well to form a soft consistency which will spoon easily. Mix in the chives and basil.
3 Halve and stone the avocados and arrange on a serving dish.
4 Spoon the soft cheese into the avocados and sprinkle with the pecan nuts. Serve immediately.

Cheddar and Garlic Lettuce Cups

These crisp lettuce heads make a deliciously different starter. It is Mexican in origin but lighter than the original version, which would include avocado pear and bacon as well as the cheese and soured cream. Reduced-fat Cheddar cheese has all the flavour but about half the fat of traditional Cheddar.

PREPARATION TIME: *15 mins*   FREEZING: *Not suitable*
COOKING TIME: —   SERVES: *4*

Imperial (Metric)	*American*
2 heads round lettuce	2 heads round lettuce
5 fl oz (150ml) carton soured cream	⅔ cup sour cream
3 spring onions	3 scallions
1 clove garlic, crushed	1 clove garlic, crushed
3 oz (75g) reduced-fat Cheddar cheese	¾ cup reduced-fat Cheddar cheese

To garnish
Snipped chives or paprika

1 Separate out the lettuce heads to extract the inner cupped leaves. Use 3 per person to build 4 cups. Arrange on serving plates.
2 Put the soured cream into a mixing bowl. Chop the spring onions (scallions) and add to the bowl with the garlic. Mix well.
3 Set aside for 10 minutes for the flavours to develop, then divide between the lettuce cups.
4 Cube the Cheddar cheese and arrange on the soured cream mixture. Sprinkle with chives or paprika and serve immediately.

Chive and Blue Cheese Dip

Serve this tangy dip with pre-dinner nibbles or add it to the buffet table. Make sure the vegetables are really fresh and full of flavour.

PREPARATION TIME: *25 mins*   FREEZING: *Not suitable*
COOKING TIME: —   SERVES: *4*

Imperial (Metric)
5 fl oz (150ml) fromage frais
2 oz (50g) Stilton or
  Roquefort cheese, grated
1 tablespoon freshly
  chopped chives
1 tablespoon semi-skimmed
  milk

American
⅔ cup fromage frais
½ cup grated Stilton or
  Roquefort cheese
1 tablespoon freshly
  chopped chives
1 tablespoon low-fat
  milk

To serve
2 carrots, cut into large sticks
2 celery stalks, cut into large
  sticks
1 large green pepper, cut
  into strips
8 baby corn

1 Put the fromage frais into a mixing bowl. Add the blue cheese and the chives. Mix well.
2 Stir in the milk. Cover and set aside for the flavours to develop. Allow a minimum of 20 minutes, but it can be prepared up to 2 hours in advance.
3 Serve with the freshly prepared vegetable crudités.

Rainbow Pepper Salad with Mackerel

This salad meal makes an ideal quick and easy starter for a special dinner party. Grilling (broiling), then skinning (bell) peppers gives them a sweeter flavour and makes them far easier to digest. Serve with wholewheat bread.

PREPARATION TIME: *5 mins*   FREEZING: *Not suitable*
COOKING TIME: *5–7 mins*   SERVES: *4*

Imperial (Metric)	American
1 red pepper	1 red bell pepper
1 green pepper	1 green bell pepper
1 yellow pepper	1 yellow bell pepper
8 oz (225g) smoked mackerel	2 cups smoked mackerel
½ red-skinned onion, sliced	½ red-skinned onion, sliced

For the dressing	**For the dressing**
Grated rind and juice of 1 lime	Grated rind and juice of 1 lime
1 tablespoon freshly chopped parsley	1 tablespoon freshly chopped parsley
2 tablespoons olive oil	2 tablespoons olive oil
1 tablespoon white wine vinegar	1 tablespoon white wine vinegar
Freshly ground black pepper	Freshly ground black pepper

1 Cut each (bell) pepper in half lengthways, then remove and discard the seeds.
2 Grill (broil) the (bell) peppers, skin side up, until the skins blister and blacken. Set aside to cool, then peel – this is very easy and much quicker than it sounds.
3 Cut the skinned peppers into thin strips and place in a mixing bowl. Flake the mackerel and add to the bowl with the sliced onion.
4 Prepare the dressing: put the lime rind and juice into a small bowl with the parsley, olive oil, vinegar and a seasoning of pepper. Whisk to combine.
5 Pour the dressing over the salad. Toss to combine. Set aside for 15 minutes then serve on plates.

Green Pasta with Baby Corn

Green pasta is flavoured with spinach. This quick starter or snack meal is delicious served with warm French bread to mop up the juices.

PREPARATION TIME: *10 mins* FREEZING: *Not suitable*
COOKING TIME: *10 mins* SERVES: *6*

Imperial (Metric)	*American*
12 oz (350g) green pasta shapes	6 cups green pasta shapes
2 tablespoons walnut oil	2 tablespoons walnut oil
1 tablespoon sunflower seeds	1 tablespoon sunflower seeds
2 tablespoons sunflower oil	2 tablespoons sunflower oil
8 oz (225g) fresh baby sweetcorn	2 cups baby corn
Juice of ½ lime	Juice of ½ lime
A little sea salt and freshly ground black pepper	A little sea salt and freshly ground black pepper

1 Cook the pasta in a large pan of boiling water for 8 minutes, or until *al dente*, then drain and return to the pan with the walnut oil. Toss to coat. Set aside and keep warm.
2 Meanwhile, quickly dry-fry the sunflower seeds in a non-stick frying pan (skillet), stirring frequently, until lightly toasted. Turn on to a plate and set aside.
3 Heat the sunflower oil in the frying pan (skillet) and stir-fry the baby corn for 2–3 minutes, until tender-crisp.
4 Add the contents of the pan to the pasta with the lime juice and a seasoning of sea salt and black pepper.
5 Toss lightly and serve immediately, sprinkled with the toasted sunflower seeds.

Courgette and Prawn Soup

This quick-to-cook soup has a wonderful flavour. The quickest way to prepare the vegetables is to slice them on the food processor.

PREPARATION TIME: *15 mins*   FREEZING: *Suitable at end of stage 6*
COOKING TIME: *25 mins*   SERVES: *4*

Imperial (Metric)	American
1 lb (450g) courgettes	1 pound zucchini
1 medium potato	1 medium potato
1 oz (25g) butter	2 tablespoons butter
2 pints (1.2 litres) vegetable or fish stock	5 cups vegetable or fish stock
2 tablespoons freshly chopped chives	2 tablespoons freshly chopped chives
4 oz (100g) frozen peas, defrosted	1 cup frozen peas, defrosted
2 tablespoons soy sauce	2 tablespoons soy sauce
4 oz (100g) peeled prawns	½ cup peeled prawns

1 Trim and thinly slice the courgettes (zucchini). Peel and dice the potato.
2 Melt the butter in a large saucepan and sauté the vegetables for 5 minutes before stirring in the stock and chives.
3 Bring to the boil, then cover and simmer for 15 minutes, until the vegetables are tender.
4 Using a draining spoon, lift the vegetables into a food processor. Add about 10 fl oz (300ml/1¼ cups) of the cooking liquid and process until smooth.
5 Carefully stir the purée back into the saucepan, blending well.
6 Add the peas and soy sauce. Return to the boil and simmer for 2 minutes. Remove from the heat.
7 Stir in the prawns (shrimps) and reheat gently, without boiling. Serve immediately.

Spinach and Potato Soup

A creamy, filling soup with a good flavour. Ideal to take on picnics in a thermos flask or to serve as a snack lunch with bread rolls and cheese. Plenty of fibre and vitamins.

PREPARATION TIME: *10 mins*   FREEZING: *Suitable*
COOKING TIME: *20 mins*   SERVES: *4–6*

Imperial (Metric)	American
2 medium potatoes	2 medium potatoes
1 medium onion	1 medium onion
8 oz (225g) frozen chopped spinach leaf	2 cups frozen chopped spinach leaf
1 pint (600ml) vegetable stock	2½ cups vegetable stock
1 clove garlic, crushed	1 clove garlic, crushed
1 teaspoon dried mixed herbs	1 teaspoon dried mixed herbs
A little sea salt and freshly ground black pepper	A little sea salt and freshly ground black pepper
10 fl oz (300ml) semi-skimmed milk	1¼ cups low-fat milk

1 Peel and dice the potatoes and onion then put them into a large pan with the frozen spinach, stock, garlic and herbs.
2 Bring to the boil. Cover and simmer for 15–20 minutes, until the potato is tender.
3 Purée the soup in a food processor.
4 Return the soup to the pan and season to taste. Stir in the milk. Reheat gently to serve.

Stilton and Celery Soup

A little Stilton goes a long way in adding a rich, unique taste to this tangy celery soup. Traditionally served at Christmas, this is also good in the summer months when you want a substantial starter before a salad main course.

PREPARATION TIME: *10 mins*   FREEZING: *Suitable at end of stage 6*
COOKING TIME: *25 mins*   SERVES: *4–6*

Imperial (Metric)	American
1 medium onion	1 medium onion
4 celery stalks	4 celery stalks
1 oz (25g) polyunsaturated margarine	2 tablespoons polyunsaturated margarine
1 clove garlic, crushed	1 clove garlic, crushed
1 oz (25g) wholewheat flour	¼ cup wholewheat flour
1¼ pints (750ml) vegetable stock	3 cups vegetable stock
2 oz (50g) Stilton cheese, grated	½ cup grated Stilton cheese
7 fl oz (200ml) reduced-fat evaporated milk	¾ cup reduced-fat evaporated milk
Freshly ground black pepper	Freshly ground black pepper

To garnish
Freshly chopped chives, celery leaves

1 Peel and chop the onion. Chop the celery.
2 Melt the margarine in a large saucepan. Add the onion, celery and garlic and sauté for 7 minutes, until the vegetables soften.
3 Stir in the flour and cook for 1 minute. Remove from the heat.
4 Blend in the stock. Bring to the boil, stirring. Cover and simmer for 20 minutes.
5 Pour into a food processor and process until smooth.

Return to the pan. Stir in the cheese and the evaporated milk.

6 Reheat gently, stirring, until the cheese melts. Season to taste with black pepper.

7 Serve immediately, garnished with the chopped chives and celery leaves.

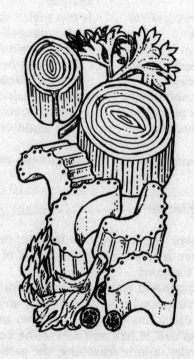

Florida Cocktail

Tangy citrus fruits bursting with vitamin C look very attractive arranged on shredded frisée lettuce with prawns (shrimps).

PREPARATION TIME: *30 mins*   FREEZING: *Not suitable*
COOKING TIME: —   SERVES: *4*

Imperial (Metric)	*American*
6 oz (175g) peeled prawns	¾ cup peeled shrimps
2 large oranges	2 large oranges
1 pink grapefruit	1 pink grapefruit
1 tablespoon freshly chopped parsley	1 tablespoon freshly chopped parsley
A little sea salt and freshly ground black pepper	A little sea salt and freshly ground black pepper
1 clove garlic, crushed (optional)	1 clove garlic, crushed (optional)
2 tablespoons sunflower oil	2 tablespoons sunflower oil

To serve
Shredded frisée lettuce

1 Put the prawns (shrimps) into a large mixing bowl. Using a zester, remove the zest from half of one orange and add to the bowl.
2 Peel the oranges and grapefruit then, holding the fruit over the mixing bowl so that you catch any juice, segment it, discarding the pith and inner membranes. Cut each segment in half and add to the bowl.
3 Add the parsley, a little seasoning, the garlic, if using, and the sunflower oil. Toss to coat.
4 Cover and refrigerate for about 15 minutes for the flavours to mingle.
5 Arrange the lettuce on 4 plates, top with the prawn (shrimp) and fruit mixture and serve immediately, spooning over any of the juices left in the mixing bowl.

MAIN MEALS IN MINUTES

With today's hectic lifestyle, it's not always easy to present a nutritionally balanced main meal fairly quickly. There are seventeen such dishes in this varied chapter and accompaniments requiring the minimum of effort are suggested for each recipe. As bread is pretty instant, keep a supply of various breads and rolls in the freezer – rye, wholewheat and granary, along with wholewheat muffins and crumpets, are all useful, as they can be defrosted and reheated quickly.

Main-Meal Vegetable Broth

A bowl of hot soup is welcome as a snack at almost any time. This soup is particularly filling and makes a good main meal when served with wholewheat rolls and low-fat cheese or some vegetable pâté.

PREPARATION TIME: *10 mins*   FREEZING: *Suitable*
COOKING TIME: *35 mins*   SERVES: *4*

Imperial (Metric)	American
3 young carrots	3 young carrots
2 young parsnips	2 young parsnips
3 celery stalks	3 celery stalks
2 leeks	2 leeks
2 tablespoons sunflower oil	2 tablespoons sunflower oil
2 bay leaves	2 bay leaves
2 pints (1.2 litres) vegetable stock	5 cups vegetable stock
A little sea salt and freshly ground black pepper	A little sea salt and freshly ground black pepper
15 oz (125g) can butter beans, drained	15-ounce can lima beans, drained
1 oz (25g) rolled oats	¼ cup rolled oats

1 Peel and dice the carrots and parsnips. Chop the celery and slice the leeks.
2 Heat the oil in a large saucepan, then sauté the carrots, parsnips, celery and leeks for about 7 minutes, until softened.
3 Add the bay leaves. Pour in the stock and season lightly with the salt and pepper.
4 Bring to the boil then simmer, covered, for approximately 25 minutes, until the vegetables are tender.
5 Stir in the butter (lima) beans and oats and simmer for 1–2 minutes, then serve.

Smoked Trout and Red Kidney Bean Salad

Canned beans are quick to use, they are also a good source of energy and protein without being too high in calories. The trout provides vitamins A and D and polyunsaturated fat.

Serve with a green salad and baked potatoes or French bread.

PREPARATION TIME: *10 mins*   FREEZING: *Not suitable*
COOKING TIME: —   SERVES: *4*

Imperial (Metric)	*American*
2 celery stalks	2 celery stalks
3 spring onions	3 scallions
2 medium tomatoes	2 medium tomatoes
2 oz (50g) watercress, roughly chopped	1 cup roughly chopped watercress
15 oz (425g) can red kidney beans	15-ounce can red kidney beans
7 oz (200g) can sweetcorn, drained	7-ounce can corn kernels, drained
12 oz (350g) smoked trout	2 cups smoked trout

For the dressing

2 tablespoons olive oil	2 tablespoons olive oil
1 clove garlic, crushed	1 clove garlic, crushed
2 tablespoons red wine vinegar	2 tablespoons red wine vinegar
1 teaspoon Worcestershire sauce	1 teaspoon Worcestershire sauce
1 teaspoon dried parsley	1 teaspoon dried parsley
A little sea salt and freshly ground black pepper	A little sea salt and freshly ground black pepper

1 Chop the celery and slice the spring onions (scallions). Chop the tomatoes.
2 Put the celery into a large mixing bowl with the spring onions (scallions) and the watercress.

3 Drain and rinse the red kidney beans and add to the bowl with the sweetcorn and tomatoes.

4 Make the dressing: put the olive oil into a small bowl with the garlic, red wine vinegar, Worcestershire sauce and parsley. Season with a little salt and pepper. Whisk lightly with a fork.

5 Pour the dressing over the salad. Toss to mix and turn on to a serving platter.

6 Flake the trout, discarding the skin and bones, and arrange evenly over the salad. Serve immediately.

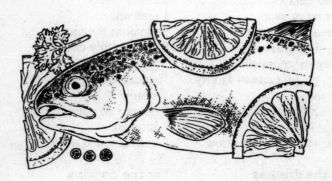

Pasta with Corn and Tomatoes

Quorn is a vegetable protein, with no cholesterol, and a little goes a long way in this healthy pasta dish. Delicious on its own or serve with French bread and a mixed salad.

PREPARATION TIME: *15 mins*   FREEZING: *Not suitable*
COOKING TIME: *15 mins*   SERVES: *4*

Imperial (Metric)	American
12 oz (350g) wholewheat pasta shells	6 cups wholewheat pasta shells
1 tablespoon + 1 teaspoon sunflower oil	1 tablespoon + 1 teaspoon sunflower oil
1 onion	1 onion
9 oz (250g) cubed Quorn (vegetable protein)	2 cups cubed Quorn (vegetable protein)
2 cloves garlic, crushed	2 cloves garlic, crushed
1 teaspoon dried oregano	1 teaspoon dried oregano
14 oz (400g) can chopped tomatoes	14-ounce can chopped tomatoes
2 tablespoons tomato paste	2 tablespoons tomato paste
4 fl oz (120ml) vegetable stock	½ cup vegetable stock
200g (7 oz) can sweetcorn, drained	7-ounce can corn kernels, drained
2 oz (50g) Mozzarella cheese, thinly sliced	½ cup thinly sliced Mozzarella cheese

1 Cook the pasta in a large pan of boiling water with the teaspoon of corn oil for approximately 10 minutes or until *al dente*.
2 Meanwhile, peel and chop the onion. Heat the remaining sunflower oil in a large frying pan (skillet) and sauté the Quorn, onion and garlic for about 5 minutes.
3 Add the oregano, tomatoes and tomato paste to the pan with the stock. Bring to the boil, stirring.

4 Cover and simmer for 8 minutes, add the sweetcorn and heat through gently.
5 Drain the pasta and transfer to a warm serving dish. Cover with the sauce and serve immediately, topped with the slices of Mozzarella cheese.

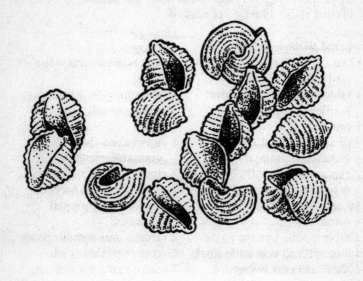

Tofu and Bean Sauté

A quickly prepared high-protein meal that's ideal for vegetarians. Tofu is readily available from healthfood shops. It's low in fat and calories and easy to digest. Serve with baked potatoes and a tossed green salad.

PREPARATION TIME: *10 mins*   FREEZING: *Not suitable*
COOKING TIME: *10 mins*   SERVES: *4*

Imperial (Metric)	*American*
1 medium onion	1 medium onion
7½ oz (210g) block smoked tofu	1 block tofu
2 tablespoons sunflower oil	2 tablespoons sunflower oil
4 oz (100g) mushrooms, sliced	1 cup sliced mushrooms
4 oz (100g) fine green beans	1 cup fine green beans
1 tablespoon wholewheat flour	1 tablespoon wholewheat flour
2 teaspoons paprika	2 teaspoons paprika
7 fl oz (200ml) vegetable stock	¾ cup vegetable stock
5 fl oz (150ml) fromage frais	⅔ cup fromage frais

To serve
Grated Parmesan cheese

1 Peel and chop the onion. Grill (broil) the block of tofu on both sides until lightly browned then cut into 1 in (2.5cm) cubes.
2 Heat the oil in a large frying pan (skillet), add the onion, mushrooms and beans and sauté for about 5 minutes, until the vegetables start to soften.
3 Stir in the flour and paprika and cook, stirring, for a further minute.
4 Add the stock. Bring to the boil, stirring, then simmer for 2 minutes.
5 Stir in the cubed tofu and the fromage frais then simmer for 5–7 minutes, until vegetables are tender.
6 Serve immediately, sprinkled with Parmesan cheese.

Quorn and Grape Fricassée

Vegetable proteins such as Quorn taste rather like chicken. They are low in fat, high in fibre and quick to use as they only need re-heating. Serve this tasty dish with a salad and warm bread rolls.

PREPARATION TIME: *10 mins*   FREEZING: *Not suitable*
COOKING TIME: *15 mins*   SERVES: *4*

Imperial (Metric)	American
8 oz (225g) easy-cook brown rice	1¼ cups easy-cook brown rice
1 medium onion	1 medium onion
1 tablespoon olive oil	1 tablespoon olive oil
3 tablespoons wholewheat flour	3 tablespoons wholewheat flour
15 fl oz (450ml) vegetable stock	2 cups vegetable stock
2 teaspoons dried parsley, or 1 tablespoon freshly chopped	2 teaspoons dried parsley, or 1 tablespoon freshly chopped
3 tablespoons single cream	3 tablespoons light cream
9 oz (250g) Quorn or other vegetable protein, cubed	2 cups cubed Quorn or other vegetable protein
8 oz (225g) seedless white grapes	1 cup seedless white grapes

1 Cook the rice in a large pan of boiling water for approximately 20–25 minutes, or as directed on the packet.
2 Meanwhile, peel and chop the onion. Heat the oil in a medium saucepan then sauté the onion for 5 minutes, until softened. Stir in the flour and cook, stirring, for 1 minute.
3 Gradually add the stock and the parsley. Bring to the boil, stirring continuously. Simmer for 2–3 minutes.
4 Remove from the heat then stir in the cream with the

- Quorn and the grapes. Heat through thoroughly, stirring.
5 Drain the rice and arrange round the edge of a warmed serving dish. Pour the fricassée into the centre of dish and serve immediately.

Chick Pea Burgers

These crunchy burgers make an excellent healthy alternative to fast-food snacks and contain plenty of protein and fibre with vitamin B. Serve them with tomato ketchup and a mixed salad.

PREPARATION TIME: *20 mins*   FREEZING: *Not suitable*
COOKING TIME: *20 mins*   SERVES: *4*

Imperial (Metric)	*American*
1 small courgette	1 small zucchini
2 spring onions	2 scallions
2 slices wholewheat bread	2 slices wholewheat bread
4 oz (100g) button mushrooms, halved	1½ cups halved button mushrooms
15 oz (425g) can chick peas, drained	15-ounce can chick peas, drained
1 egg, beaten	1 egg, beaten
Freshly ground black pepper	Freshly ground black pepper
5 tablespoons wholewheat flour	5 tablespoons wholewheat flour
3 tablespoons sunflower oil	3 tablespoons sunflower oil

1 Top, tail and slice the courgette (zucchini). Roughly chop the spring onions (scallions).
2 Tear the bread into pieces and blend into breadcrumbs in the food processor.
3 Add the spring onions (scallions) and courgette (zucchini) and process to chop. Add the mushrooms and process again until finely chopped.
4 Add the drained chick peas, the egg and a little black pepper. Process just to combine to a stiff dough.
5 Chill for 10 minutes. Turn on to a board and shape into 8 burgers. Coat them on both sides with the flour.
6 Heat the oil in a frying pan (skillet) and fry 4 burgers at a time, cooking them for 2–3 minutes on each side, until golden.
7 Drain on absorbent paper and serve immediately.

Note: For a more spicy version add 1 clove garlic and 1 teaspoon curry powder to the processor with the courgette (zucchini).

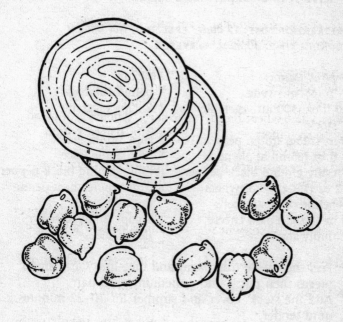

Penne with Swede (Rutabaga), Peas and Cheese

Piping hot tubes of high-fibre wholewheat pasta, topped with colourful vegetables and served with high-protein cheese – a filling meal fit for a king!

Serve with a simple mixed salad.

PREPARATION TIME: *15 mins*   FREEZING: *Not suitable*
COOKING TIME: *30 mins*   SERVES: *4*

Imperial (Metric)	American
1 lb (450g) swede	1 pound rutabaga
10 fl oz (300ml) vegetable stock	1¼ cups vegetable stock
8 oz (225g) frozen peas	2 cups frozen peas
3 fl oz (85ml) apple juice	⅓ cup apple juice
Freshly ground black pepper	Freshly ground black pepper
12 oz (350g) wholewheat penne or pasta shells	6 cups wholewheat penne or pasta shells
4 oz (100g) Edam cheese, thinly sliced	1½ cups thinly sliced Edam cheese

1 Peel the swede (rutabaga) and dice into fairly small pieces then put it into a medium-sized pan.
2 Add the stock, cover and simmer for 20–25 minutes, until tender.
3 Transfer the contents of the pan to a food processor and process until puréed.
4 Return to the pan and stir in the peas and apple juice. Season lightly with the black pepper.
5 Simmer, covered, for a further 5 minutes.
6 Meanwhile, cook the pasta in a large pan of boiling water, for 10–12 minutes, until *al dente*. Stir the pasta once or twice during cooking to prevent it sticking.
7 Drain the pasta and turn on to a warmed serving dish. Pour over the vegetable sauce. Top with the thinly sliced cheese and serve immediately. The cheese will melt as you put the dish on the table.

Chinese Vegetable and Pecan Nut Stir Fry

A colourful vegetarian dish which is full of fibre and vitamins. The pecan nuts add protein.

PREPARATION TIME: *15 mins*   FREEZING: *Not suitable*
COOKING TIME: *10–12 mins*   SERVES: *4*

Imperial (Metric)	American
6 oz (175g) egg noodles	1¼ cups egg noodles
2 red peppers	2 red bell peppers
1 bunch spring onions	1 bunch scallions
3 courgettes	3 zucchini
2 tablespoons olive oil	2 tablespoons olive oil
1 clove garlic, crushed	1 clove garlic, crushed
4 oz (100g) button mushrooms, sliced	1 cup sliced button mushrooms
Rind and juice of 1 orange	Rind and juice of 1 orange
2 tablespoons medium sherry	2 tablespoons medium sherry
2 oz (50g) pecan nuts, chopped	½ cup chopped pecan nuts

1 Cook the noodles: place them in about 2 pints (1.2 litres/5 cups) boiling water, then simmer for 3–4 minutes. Break up with a fork.
2 Meanwhile deseed and slice the red (bell) peppers, chop the spring onions (scallions) and slice the courgettes (zucchini).
3 Heat the oil in a wok or large frying pan (skillet). Stir fry the garlic, (bell) peppers and spring onions (scallions) for 2 minutes.
4 Add the courgettes (zucchini) and mushrooms and cook for a further 3–4 minutes.
5 Drain the noodles and add to the vegetables with the orange rind and juice and the sherry. Heat through thoroughly, stirring gently.
6 Serve immediately, topped with the pecan nuts.

Red Kidney Bean and Cashew Hot Pot

This filling main meal can be put together pretty quickly with a few cans from the cupboard – yet it tastes delicious and is high in protein, fibre and vitamins but low on fat. Serve with boiled rice or pasta or just chunks of French bread if you're really pressed for time.

PREPARATION TIME: *15 mins*   FREEZING: *Suitable at end of stage 6*
COOKING TIME: *18 mins*   SERVES: *4*

Imperial (Metric)	American
1 onion	1 onion
1 tablespoon sunflower oil	1 tablespoon sunflower oil
1 clove garlic, crushed	1 clove garlic, crushed
6 oz (175g) button mushrooms, halved	3 cups halved button mushrooms
8 oz (225g) can red kidney beans	8-ounce can red kidney beans
15 oz (425g) can butter beans	15-ounce can lima beans
14 oz (400g) can chopped tomatoes	14-ounce can chopped tomatoes
1 tablespoon freshly chopped parsley	1 tablespoon freshly chopped parsley
4 oz (100g) frozen green beans	1 cup frozen green beans
A little sea salt and freshly ground black pepper	A little sea salt and freshly ground black pepper
1 tablespoon Worcestershire sauce	1 tablespoon Worcestershire sauce
3 oz (75g) toasted cashew nuts	⅔ cup toasted cashew nuts

1 Peel and finely chop the onion.
2 Heat the oil in a medium saucepan, then sauté the onion with the garlic for about 5 minutes, until softened.
3 Stir in the mushrooms and continue to sauté for 2–3 minutes.
4 Drain and rinse the red kidney beans and the butter (lima) beans and add to the pan. Purée the tomatoes

in a food processor and add to the pan with the
parsley and green beans.

5 Season lightly with salt and pepper. Add the
Worcestershire sauce.

6 Bring to the boil, stirring, over a medium heat.
Simmer, covered, for 5–7 minutes.

7 Serve immediately topped with the cashew nuts.

Note: To toast cashew nuts quickly and easily, spread
them out on a dinner plate and microwave on 100%
(full power) for 3–4 minutes or toast, watching carefully,
under the grill.

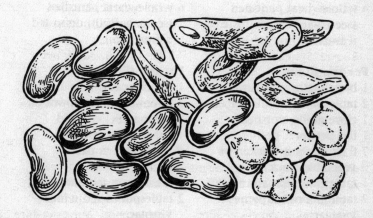

Salmon and Beansprout Pancakes

To save time, the pancakes can be made in advance and frozen. See the recipe for Blackcurrant Pancakes on page 170.

The filling has a definite taste of the Orient; it's high in protein, low in fat, colourful and tasty. A delicious, satisfying meal which needs only a green salad as an accompaniment.

PREPARATION TIME: *15 mins*   FREEZING: *Not suitable*
COOKING TIME: *25 mins*   SERVES: *4*

Imperial (Metric)	American
6 wholewheat pancakes (see page 170), defrosted if frozen	6 wholewheat pancakes (see page 170), defrosted if frozen

For the filling

1 bunch spring onions	1 bunch scallions
2 tablespoons sunflower oil	2 tablespoons sunflower oil
1 clove garlic, crushed	1 clove garlic, crushed
1 red pepper	1 red (bell) pepper
7 fl oz (200ml) chicken or vegetable stock	¾ cup chicken or vegetable stock
1 tablespoon tomato paste	1 tablespoon tomato paste
2 tablespoons red wine vinegar	2 tablespoons red wine vinegar
1 tablespoon clear honey	1 tablespoon clear honey
2 tablespoons rich soy sauce	2 tablespoons rich soy sauce
1 tablespoon wholewheat flour	1 tablespoon wholewheat flour
8 oz (225g) fresh beansprouts	8 oz (225g) fresh beansprouts
6 oz (175g) can salmon in brine, drained	6-ounce can salmon in brine, drained

1 Preheat the oven to gas mark 6, 400°F (200°C).
2 Make the filling: chop the spring onions (scallions).
   Heat the oil in a medium-sized saucepan then sauté the
   garlic with the spring onions (scallions) for 5 minutes.
3 Deseed and chop the red (bell) pepper and add to the
   pan. Continue to cook for a further 3 minutes.
4 In a small mixing bowl blend together the stock,
   tomato paste, vinegar, honey, soy sauce and flour. Stir
   into the pan.
5 Cook, stirring continuously, until the sauce boils and
   thickens.
6 Remove from the heat and stir in the beansprouts.
7 Remove the skin and bones from the salmon and flake
   into the sauce. Heat through thoroughly.
8 Divide the sauce between the pancakes, roll up and
   arrange close together in an ovenproof dish.
9 Cover with foil and bake in the preheated oven for
   about 15 minutes, until heated through. Alternatively
   the pancakes and sauce may be layered in a stack,
   covered and reheated, then served cut into wedges.

Vegetarian Pasta Supper

The Provençal sauce enhances the nutty-tasting pasta both in appearance and flavour. Serve with a tossed salad of iceberg lettuce, watercress and grated carrot for a complete meal.

PREPARATION TIME: *10 mins* FREEZING: *Not suitable*
COOKING TIME: *20 mins* SERVES: *4*

Imperial (Metric)	American
1 large green pepper	1 large green (bell) pepper
1 large onion	1 large onion
2 medium mushrooms	2 medium mushrooms
2 tablespoons + 1 teaspoon olive oil	2 tablespoons + 1 teaspoon olive oil
1 clove garlic, crushed	1 clove garlic, crushed
1 medium cauliflower, divided into florets	1 medium cauliflower, divided into florets
14 oz (400g) can chopped tomatoes with herbs	14-ounce can chopped tomatoes with herbs
2 tablespoons tomato paste	2 tablespoons tomato paste
A little sea salt and freshly ground black pepper	A little sea salt and freshly ground black pepper
10 oz (275g) wholewheat pasta shells	4¼ cups wholewheat pasta shells

To serve
Grated Parmesan cheese

1 Deseed and chop the green (bell) pepper. Chop the onion and mushrooms.
2 Prepare the sauce: heat the 2 tablespoons oil in a medium saucepan, then fry the onion, garlic and green pepper for about 5 minutes, stirring occasionally, until the onion softens.
3 Stir in the cauliflower with the mushrooms and tomatoes and the tomato paste. Season lightly with salt and pepper.

4 Bring to the boil, then simmer, covered, for 10–12 minutes, removing the lid for the last 2–3 minutes to allow the liquid to evaporate a little if necessary.

5 Meanwhile, add the pasta and the teaspoon of oil to a large saucepan of boiling water, return to the boil and simmer for 10–12 minutes, or until *al dente*.

6 Drain the pasta, top with the sauce and serve immediately, sprinkled with the Parmesan cheese.

Vegetable Stroganoff

Vegetables in a creamy-tasting yet low-fat sauce, topped with toasted sunflower seeds. A high-fibre meal with a good supply of vitamins that's suitable for vegetarians. Serve with brown rice or wholewheat pasta.

PREPARATION TIME: *15 mins*   FREEZING: *Not suitable*
COOKING TIME: *14 mins*   SERVES: *4*

Imperial (Metric)
11 oz (300g) packet fresh or frozen broccoli spears
1 large onion
4 celery stalks
2 tablespoons sunflower oil
12 oz (350g) button mushrooms, halved
3 tablespoons wholewheat flour
10 fl oz (300ml) vegetable stock
10 fl oz (300ml) semi-skimmed milk
Freshly ground black pepper

American
11-ounce packet fresh or frozen broccoli spears
1 large onion
4 celery stalks
2 tablespoons sunflower oil
6 cups button mushrooms, halved
3 tablespoons wholewheat flour
1¼ cups vegetable stock
1¼ cups low-fat milk
Freshly ground black pepper

To serve
2 tablespoons toasted sunflower seeds
1 oz (25g/1¼ cup) reduced-fat Cheddar cheese, grated

1 Defrost and roughly chop the broccoli. Peel and chop the onion then chop the celery.
2 Heat the oil in a large saucepan, then sauté the onion and celery for about 5 minutes, until the onion softens.
3 Add the broccoli and mushrooms to the pan and continue to sauté for 2 minutes.
4 Stir in the flour and cook for a further 2 minutes. Add

the stock and milk. Season lightly with black pepper.
5 Bring to the boil, stirring, then simmer uncovered for 4–5 minutes.
6 Serve on a bed of brown rice or wholewheat pasta, sprinkled with the sunflower seeds and grated cheese.

Chicken Liver and Mushroom Salad

Mushrooms and chicken livers are cooked in oil then served on a bed of mixed salad leaves, with thick slices of warm wholewheat French bread. A delicious lunch or supper dish providing protein, iron and vitamins A and D.

PREPARATION TIME: *15 mins*   FREEZING: *Not suitable*
COOKING TIME: *10 mins*   SERVES: *4*

Imperial (Metric)	*American*
For the dressing	**For the dressing**
1 tablespoon olive oil	1 tablespoon olive oil
2 teaspoons cider vinegar	2 teaspoons cider vinegar
2 tablespoons orange juice	2 tablespoons orange juice
A little sea salt and freshly ground black pepper	A little sea salt and freshly ground black pepper
½ teaspoon dried oregano	½ teaspoon dried oregano
1 clove garlic, crushed	1 clove garlic, crushed
For the salad	**For the salad**
2 Little Gem lettuces	2 Little Gem lettuces
1 small head radicchio	1 small head radicchio
1 bunch watercress	1 bunch watercress
3 tablespoons olive oil	3 tablespoons olive oil
12 oz (350g) cleaned chicken livers	2 cups cleaned chicken livers
8 oz (225g) button mushrooms, sliced	4 cups sliced button mushrooms

1 Make the dressing by combining the olive oil, cider vinegar, orange juice, seasoning, oregano and garlic in a small bowl and whisking with a fork. Set aside.
2 Tear the lettuces, radicchio and the watercress into small pieces and arrange on a large oval serving dish. Roughly chop the chicken livers.
3 Heat the oil in a frying pan (skillet) then quickly fry the chicken livers over a fairly high heat until well

browned on all sides. Drain on absorbent paper and keep warm.

4 Fry the mushrooms in the remaining oil until starting to crisp, stirring frequently. Drain on absorbent paper and keep warm.

5 Pour the dressing on to the salad leaves and toss to coat evenly.

6 Top the salad with the chicken livers and mushrooms and serve immediately.

Speedy Paella

Rice is a valuable carbohydrate food and brown rice is a rich source of the B group of vitamins.

This quick and easy paella dish is best served piping hot with just a tossed mixed salad or a bowl of black and green olives.

PREPARATION TIME: *15 mins*   FREEZING: *Not suitable*
COOKING TIME: *25 mins*   SERVES: *4*

Imperial (Metric)	American
2 medium onions or 1 large	2 medium onions or 1 large
1 medium green pepper	1 medium green bell pepper
2 tablespoons sunflower oil	2 tablespoons sunflower oil
2 cloves garlic, crushed	2 cloves garlic, crushed
8 oz (225g) skinned and boned chicken breast	1 cup skinned and boned chicken breast
8 oz (225g) easy-cook brown rice	1¼ cups easy-cook brown rice
1 pint (600ml) chicken or vegetable stock	2½ cups chicken or vegetable stock
½ teaspoon turmeric	½ teaspoon turmeric
6 oz (175g) frozen peas	1½ cups frozen peas
8 oz (225g) peeled prawns	1 cup peeled shrimps
2 tablespoons freshly chopped parsley	2 tablespoons freshly chopped parsley

To garnish
Wedges of lemon

1 Peel and chop the onions. Deseed and chop the green (bell) pepper.
2 Heat the oil in a large frying pan (skillet) or a paella pan. Add the onion, green (bell) pepper and garlic and fry, stirring frequently, until the onion softens and turns golden brown.
3 Remove the vegetables, using a draining spoon. Set aside.

4 Cut the chicken into thin strips and add to the pan. Brown quickly on all sides over a fairly high heat.
5 Return the onion and green pepper to the pan with the rice. Stir to coat the rice with oil, over a low heat.
6 Add the stock and turmeric. Bring to a rapid boil, then cover and simmer for 20 minutes or until the rice is almost tender and most of the liquid has been absorbed.
7 Add the peas, cover and simmer for a further 5 minutes.
8 Stir in the prawns (shrimps) and parsley and reheat briefly, stirring. Serve immediately garnished with the wedges of lemon.

Chicken and Mango Pilaff

Cooked rice keeps in the refrigerator for up to 5 days if well covered. After cooking, rinse it well, in a sieve under cold running water, then drain and store.

This dish can be put together quickly yet is very nutritious and looks good enough for entertaining.

PREPARATION TIME: *20 mins*   FREEZING: *Not suitable*
COOKING TIME: *10 mins*   SERVES: *4*

Imperial (Metric)	American
2 celery stalks	2 celery stalks
1 red pepper	1 red bell pepper
½ mango	½ mango
2 tablespoons sunflower oil	2 tablespoons sunflower oil
8 oz (225g) boneless chicken breast, skinned and thinly sliced	1 cup skinned and thinly sliced boneless chicken breast
8 oz (225g) cabbage, shredded	2 cups shredded cabbage
10 oz (275g) cooked brown rice	1¾ cups cooked brown rice
Rind and juice of 1 orange	Rind and juice of 1 orange
A little sea salt and freshly ground black pepper	A little sea salt and freshly ground black pepper

1 Chop the celery stalks. Deseed and chop the red (bell) pepper, then peel and stone the mango and cut into cubes.
2 Heat the oil in a wok or large frying pan (skillet) then sauté the chicken over a fairly high heat for about 5 minutes, until browned on all sides. Remove, using a draining spoon, and keep warm.
3 Add the celery, red (bell) pepper and cabbage to the pan and sauté for a further 3 minutes until the vegetables soften slightly and take on bright colours.
4 Return the chicken to the pan with the mango, rice and orange rind and juice. Season slightly. Reheat thoroughly, stirring, and serve immediately.

Creamy Vegetable and Prawn Curry

A creamy curry that is low in fat as the sauce is made from reduced-fat evaporated milk. This dish is rich in protein, fibre and vitamins. Serve with brown rice or wholewheat pitta bread and salad.

PREPARATION TIME: *10 mins*   FREEZING: *Not suitable*
COOKING TIME: *24 mins*   SERVES: *4*

Imperial (Metric)	American
2 medium carrots	2 medium carrots
1 onion	1 onion
1 celery stalk	1 celery stalk
2 tablespoons sunflower oil	2 tablespoons sunflower oil
1 tablespoon medium curry powder	1 tablespoon medium curry powder
2 tablespoons wholewheat flour	2 tablespoons wholewheat flour
5 fl oz (150ml) vegetable stock	⅔ cup vegetable stock
14 oz (400g) can reduced-fat evaporated milk	14-ounce can reduced-fat evaporated milk
1 medium-sized eating apple	1 medium-sized eating apple
1 teaspoon dried parsley or 1 tablespoon freshly chopped	1 teaspoon dried parsley or 1 tablespoon freshly chopped
6 oz (175g) frozen baby sweetcorn, halved	1⅓ cups halved frozen baby corn
4 oz (100g) frozen peas	1 cup frozen peas
8 oz (225g) peeled prawns	1 cup peeled shrimps

1 Scrub and dice the carrots. Peel and chop the onion and chop the celery.
2 Heat the oil in a large saucepan, then sauté the onion, carrots and celery over a medium heat for about 5 minutes, until the onion softens.
3 Stir in the curry powder with the flour and cook, stirring, over a low heat for 2 minutes.

4 Gradually add the vegetable stock and evaporated milk, stirring.
5 Core and chop the apple and add to the pan with the parsley. Bring to the boil, cover and simmer gently for 10 minutes. Add the baby corn and peas.
6 Return to the boil, cover and simmer for 5 minutes.
7 Stir in the prawns (shrimps). Heat through and then serve immediately with rice or pitta bread.

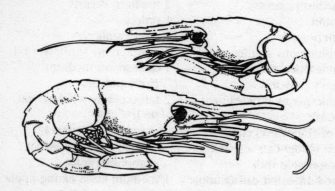

Oriental Microwave Chicken

Chicken is excellent cooked on a rack in the microwave, and it's very quick too. Brushing with this Oriental marinade before cooking means it will have a good brown colour when removed from the microwave. If you want to crisp the skin, put the chicken into a preheated hot oven for 10 minutes, after the standing time, or alternatively brown it under the grill. Serve with wholewheat noodles and a sauce made by heating a can of puréed chopped tomatoes with herbs.

PREPARATION TIME: *25 mins*   FREEZING: *Suitable*
COOKING TIME: *35 mins, including standing*   SERVES: *4*

Imperial (Metric)	*American*
3½ lb (1.5kg) chicken	3½ pound chicken

For the marinade

2 tablespoons olive oil	2 tablespoons olive oil
2 tablespoons soy sauce	2 tablespoons soy sauce
2 teaspoons clear honey	2 teaspoons clear honey
½ teaspoon dried basil	½ teaspoon dried basil
1 tablespoon tomato paste	1 tablespoon tomato paste

1 Stand the chicken on a rack or upturned saucer in a suitable dish. Secure the legs with string or an elastic band.
2 Mix together the olive oil, soy sauce, honey, basil and tomato paste. Brush this mixture all over the chicken. If you have time, set aside for 20 minutes for the flavours to penetrate.
3 Put the chicken into a roasting bag. Seal, then make a small hole in the base of the bag.
4 Microwave the chicken on 100% (full power), allowing approximately 7 minutes per pound.
5 Remove the chicken from the microwave. Cover with a tent of foil and leave to stand for 15 minutes before serving.

SALADS AND VEGETABLE DISHES

Amongst these salads and vegetable dishes you will find many varied recipes, including some that extend healthy salads and vegetables into light main meals by combining them with other ingredients, such as Macaroni au Gratin Special on page 67.

Salad leaves are fresh and summery and a selection arranged on a large oval platter looks very pretty on a buffet table. Add nuts, vegetables or pulses (legumes) for texture, as salad leaves consist mainly of water. Remember not to dress the salad until you are ready to serve as the acid and oil in the dressing causes salad leaves to wilt quickly. Try the Royal Salad on page 76 for a delicious combination of leaves with cottage cheese, fresh pineapple and dates.

For speedy buffets try serving three of the salads with a variety of low-fat cheeses accompanied by some canned fish. Warm French bread will make the meal complete. For dessert, what could be better than a colourful bowl of fruits in season? Offer a few unusual ones for a treat such as fresh dates or figs, mangoes, passion fruit, fresh pineapple etc.

Macaroni Au Gratin Special

Pasta is a valuable carbohydrate food, providing a slow release of energy, and is therefore popular with athletes, particularly before a race. This quick snack takes on the flavour of the asparagus and avocado and is delicious at any time of the year. Serve with garlic bread.

PREPARATION TIME: *15 mins*   FREEZING: *Not suitable*
COOKING TIME: *35 mins*   SERVES: *4*

Imperial (Metric)	*American*
10 oz (275g) short-cut macaroni	4¼ cups short-cut macaroni
1 large avocado	1 large avocado
12 oz (350g) can asparagus spears	12-ounce can asparagus spears

For the sauce

1 oz (25g) butter	2 tablespoons butter
2 tablespoons wholewheat flour	2 tablespoons wholewheat flour
10 fl oz (300ml) semi-skimmed milk	1¼ cups low-fat milk
2 oz (50g) reduced-fat Cheddar cheese, grated	½ cup grated reduced-fat Cheddar cheese
A little cayenne pepper	A little cayenne pepper

For the topping

1 oz (25g) wholewheat breadcrumbs	½ cup wholewheat breadcrumbs
2 oz (50g) reduced-fat Cheddar cheese, grated	½ cup grated reduced-fat Cheddar cheese
1 oz (25g) pecan nuts, chopped	3 tablespoons chopped pecan nuts

1 Preheat the oven to gas mark 6, 400°F (200°C).
2 Cook the pasta in plenty of boiling water for 7–8 minutes, until just tender.

3 Drain the pasta and transfer to a lightly greased gratin dish. Peel, stone and dice the avocado and add to the pasta. Drain and roughly chop the asparagus and add to the dish.

4 Make the sauce: melt the butter in a saucepan. Stir in the flour and cook over a medium heat for 1 minute. Stir in the milk gradually.

5 Bring to the boil, stirring, then simmer for 1–2 minutes, stirring until thickened.

6 Remove from the heat and stir in the cheese and cayenne pepper. Pour the sauce over the pasta and vegetables, to coat.

7 To make the topping, combine the breadcrumbs with the cheese and nuts. Sprinkle over the pasta dish.

8 Bake for 15–20 minutes, until golden. Serve immediately.

Pasta and Olive Salad

Pasta is an easily digested carbohydrate or high-energy food. This recipe uses wholewheat pasta, which is high in fibre and a reasonable source of iron and the B group of vitamins. Mixed with colourful (bell) peppers and olives, this pasta salad will be popular with almost everyone.

PREPARATION TIME: *10 mins* FREEZING: *Not suitable*
COOKING TIME: *14 mins* SERVES: *4*

Imperial (Metric)
10 oz (275g) wholewheat
  pasta shells
4 oz (100g) pimento-stuffed
  olives, halved
½ red pepper
½ green pepper

For the dressing
2 tablespoons cider vinegar
3 tablespoons olive oil
1 clove garlic, crushed
1 tablespoon light soy sauce

To garnish
2 tablespoons freshly
  chopped basil or parsley

American
4¼ cups wholewheat
  pasta shells
⅔ cup halved, pimento-
  stuffed olives
½ red bell pepper
½ green bell pepper

For the dressing
2 tablespoons cider vinegar
3 tablespoons olive oil
1 clove garlic, crushed
1 tablespoon light soy sauce

1 Cook the pasta in plenty of boiling water for about 10–12 minutes or until *al dente.*
2 Meanwhile make the dressing. Put all the ingredients for the dressing into a jug and whisk with a fork.
3 Drain the pasta and turn into a large salad bowl while still warm. Add the olives. Deseed and chop the red and green (bell) peppers, add to pasta. Toss lightly.
4 Pour the dressing over the pasta and toss again. Sprinkle over the parsley or basil. Serve warm or cold.

Cauliflower and Avocado Bake

This quick and easy vegetarian dish uses a sauce made by the one-stage method. Serve with a mixed salad and a good old can of baked beans!

PREPARATION TIME: *15 mins*   FREEZING: *Not suitable*
COOKING TIME: *35 mins*   SERVES: *4–6*

Imperial (Metric)
1 large cauliflower, florets
  only
1 large or 2 small avocado
  pears
Juice of ½ lemon

For the sauce
1 pint (600ml) semi-
  skimmed milk
1½ oz (40g) polyunsaturated
  margarine
1½ oz (40g) wholewheat
  flour
3 oz (75g) reduced-fat mature
  Cheddar cheese, grated
Freshly ground black pepper
1 teaspoon wholegrain
  mustard
½ teaspoon paprika

American
1 large cauliflower, florets
  only
1 large or 2 small avocado
  pears
Juice of ½ lemon

For the sauce
2½ cups low-fat
  milk
3 tablespoons
  polyunsaturated margarine
2 tablespoons wholewheat
  flour
⅔ cup grated reduced-fat
  mature Cheddar cheese
Freshly ground black pepper
1 teaspoon wholegrain
  mustard
½ teaspoon paprika

1 Preheat the oven to gas mark 6, 400°F (200°C).
2 Cook the cauliflower florets in a pan of boiling water
   for about 5 minutes, until just tender, then drain.
3 Peel, stone and roughly chop the avocado and arrange
   in a casserole dish. Sprinkle with the lemon juice. Add
   the cauliflower.
4 Prepare the sauce: put the milk, margarine and flour
   into a saucepan. Heat gently, stirring, until the
   margarine melts, then bring to the boil, stirring

70   FAST AND HEALTHY FAMILY COOKING

continuously with a balloon whisk. Boil for 1-2 minutes, stirring. Remove from the heat.

5 Stir in 2 oz (50g) of the Cheddar cheese and the black pepper and mustard. Continue stirring until the cheese melts. Pour over the cauliflower and avocado.

6 Sprinkle the remaining Cheddar cheese and the paprika over. Bake for 20-25 minutes until bubbling round the edges. Serve immediately.

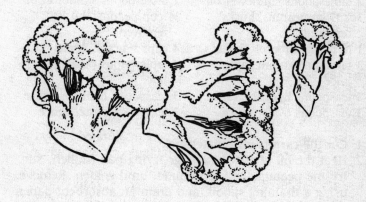

Stir-Fried Vegetables with Peanuts

Vegetables quickly cooked and served with the pan juices are high in vitamins and look and taste wonderful. Peanuts add protein to this Chinese-style vegetable dish.

PREPARATION TIME: *15 mins*   FREEZING: *Not suitable*
COOKING TIME: *10 mins*   SERVES: *4*

Imperial (Metric)	American
4 medium carrots	4 medium carrots
2 tablespoons sunflower oil	2 tablespoons sunflower oil
3oz (75g) peanuts, husks removed	⅓ cup peanuts, husks removed
1 lb (450g) broccoli florets	4 cups broccoli florets
3 tablespoons pineapple juice	3 tablespoons pineapple juice
3 teaspoons light soy sauce	3 teaspoons light soy sauce
3 teaspoons oyster sauce	3 teaspoons oyster sauce

1 Cut the carrots into matchsticks.
2 Heat the oil in a wok or large frying pan (skillet). Stir fry the peanuts for 1–2 minutes, until golden. Remove, using a draining spoon, and drain on absorbent paper.
3 Meanwhile, parboil the broccoli for 3 minutes, drain, set aside and keep warm.
4 Add the carrots to the pan and stir-fry over a medium heat for 3 minutes.
5 Blend together the pineapple juice, soy sauce and oyster sauce. Add to the carrots with the broccoli. Bring to the boil, stirring. Simmer for 1–2 minutes.
6 Stir in the nuts and serve immediately.

Ratatouille

This quick-to-prepare ratatouille makes an ideal sauce to serve over pasta for a healthy, low-calorie lunch or supper dish. It is also good served cold with salad dishes and improves if kept in the refrigerator overnight.

PREPARATION TIME: *15 mins* FREEZING: *Suitable at end of stage 4*
COOKING TIME: *35 mins* SERVES: *4*

Imperial (Metric)	American
2 large onions	2 large onions
1 lb (450g) courgettes	1 pound zucchini
1 small aubergine	1 small eggplant
2 tablespoons sunflower oil	2 tablespoons sunflower oil
2 cloves garlic, crushed	2 cloves garlic, crushed
2 red or green peppers	2 red or green bell peppers
14 oz (400g) can tomatoes	14-ounce can tomatoes
1 teaspoon dried oregano	1 teaspoon dried oregano
A little sea salt and freshly ground black pepper	A little sea salt and freshly ground black pepper
2 tablespoons freshly chopped parsley	2 tablespoons freshly chopped parsley

1 Peel and chop the onions. Slice the courgettes (zucchini), deseed and slice the (bell) peppers and dice the aubergine.
2 Heat the oil in a large pan, then sauté the onions and garlic for approximately 5 minutes, until the onions soften.
3 Add the peppers to the pan with the courgettes (zucchini) and aubergine (eggplant). Fry for a further 2 minutes, stirring.
4 Stir in the tomatoes and oregano. Season with salt and pepper. Simmer, covered, for 20 minutes. Remove the lid and boil fairly fast for 5 minutes.
5 Sprinkle with the chopped parsley and serve.

Sunny Vegetables Mediterranean Style

This Greek-type vegetable dish can be served hot or cold. If serving cold, try mixing in 2 tablespoons plain yogurt before serving.

PREPARATION TIME: *10 mins*   FREEZING: *Not suitable*
COOKING TIME: *32 mins*   SERVES: *4*

Imperial (Metric)	American
2 spring onions	2 scallions
1 small aubergine	1 small eggplant
3 young carrots	3 young carrots
1 tablespoon sunflower oil	1 tablespoon sunflower oil
1 clove garlic, crushed	1 clove garlic, crushed
14 oz (400g) can chopped tomatoes	14-ounce can chopped tomatoes
1 teaspoon tomato paste	1 teaspoon tomato paste
A little sea salt and freshly ground black pepper	A little sea salt and freshly ground black pepper
1 teaspoon dried oregano	1 teaspoon dried oregano
3 fl oz (85ml) water	⅓ cup water

To garnish
2 oz (50g/½ cup) pitted
  black olives

1 Chop the spring onions (scallions) and cube the aubergine (eggplant). Scrub and dice the carrots.
2 Heat the oil in a large saucepan, then fry the spring onions (scallions) and garlic, stirring, for 2 minutes. Add the tomatoes and tomato paste, then season with salt and pepper.
3 Add the oregano, aubergine (eggplant), carrots and water. Cover and cook very gently for 25–30 minutes, stirring occasionally, until the aubergine (eggplant) and carrots are tender but still firm.
4 Allow to stand, covered, for 5 minutes before serving garnished with the olives.

Curried Potatoes with Peas

This vegetable dish is delicious served with curries or cold chicken. It's also good as a hot dish on a buffet table, accompanied by naan bread and plain yoghurt.

PREPARATION TIME: *20 mins*   FREEZING: *Not suitable*
COOKING TIME: *30 mins*   SERVES: *4*

Imperial (Metric)	American
1½ lb (675g) waxy potatoes	1½ pounds waxy potatoes
1 medium onion	1 medium onion
¾ in (2cm) piece root ginger	¾ inch piece root ginger
2 tablespoons olive oil	2 tablespoons olive oil
1 clove garlic, crushed	1 clove garlic, crushed
14 oz (400g) can chopped tomatoes	14-ounce can chopped tomatoes
1 teaspoon lemon juice	1 teaspoon lemon juice
5 fl oz (150ml) vegetable stock	⅔ cup vegetable stock
1 teaspoon garam masala	1 teaspoon garam masala
1 teaspoon turmeric	1 teaspoon turmeric
½ teaspoon chilli powder	½ teaspoon chile powder
8 oz (225g) frozen peas	2 cups frozen peas

To garnish
Freshly chopped mint

1 Peel the potatoes and cut into ¾ in (2cm) pieces. Peel and chop the onion then peel and grate the root ginger.
2 Heat the oil in a large saucepan. Add the onion, garlic and ginger and cook over a medium heat, stirring occasionally, for 5 minutes.
3 Stir in all the remaining ingredients except the peas. Bring to the boil, cover and simmer for 15–20 minutes.
4 Add the peas, return to the boil and simmer, uncovered, for a further 5 minutes, until some of the liquid has evaporated.
5 Serve immediately, sprinkled with the chopped mint.

Royal Salad

This makes an ideal starter for 4 people or will serve 2 as a main meal. Quick and easy to prepare and pretty to look at, it is best made just before you are ready to eat. Serve the dressing separately.

PREPARATION TIME: *15 mins*   FREEZING: *Not suitable*
COOKING TIME: —   SERVES: *2–4*

Imperial (Metric)	American
4 radicchio leaves	4 radicchio leaves
½ pineapple	½ pineapple
½ Chinese cabbage	½ Chinese cabbage
8 young spinach leaves	8 young spinach leaves
4 oz (100g) beansprouts	1½ cups beansprouts
6 oz (175g) cottage cheese	¾ cup cottage cheese
4 oz (100g) stoned dates	⅔ cup stoned dates

For the dressing

1 spring onion, roughly chopped	1 scallion, roughly chopped
3 tablespoons cider vinegar	3 tablespoons cider vinegar
3 tablespoons olive oil	3 tablespoons olive oil
2 sprigs parsley	2 sprigs parsley
1 tablespoon wine mustard	1 tablespoon wine mustard

1 Put all the ingredients for the dressing into a blender and blend until smooth. Pour into a jug and set aside.
2 Shred the radicchio leaves. Peel, core and chop the pineapple. Shred the Chinese cabbage.
3 Arrange the salad leaves on individual plates. Add the beansprouts and pineapple. Place some cottage cheese in the centre of each salad. Decorate with dates and serve immediately with the dressing.

Curried Kidney Bean and Corn Salad

A colourful, high-fibre salad with a light and tangy dressing. Serve with any cold dish.

PREPARATION TIME: *10 mins*   FREEZING: *Not suitable*
COOKING TIME: *3–5 mins*   SERVES: *4*

Imperial (Metric)	American
1 green pepper	1 green pepper
6 oz (175g) frozen sweetcorn	1½ cups frozen corn kernels
15 oz (425g) can red kidney beans	15-ounce can red kidney beans
1 eating apple	1 eating apple

For the dressing

2 teaspoons medium Madras curry powder	2 teaspoons medium Madras curry powder
3 tablespoons orange juice	3 tablespoons orange juice
Grated rind of ½ orange	Grated rind of ½ orange
1 tablespoon olive oil	1 tablespoon olive oil
Freshly ground black pepper	Freshly ground black pepper
1 tablespoon freshly chopped parsley	1 tablespoon freshly chopped parsley

1 Deseed and chop the green (bell) pepper.
2 Put the sweetcorn into a suitable container, cover and microwave on 100% (full power) for 3 minutes. Stir. Alternatively, cook sweetcorn in boiling water for 5 minutes. Drain. Turn into a serving dish.
3 Drain and rinse the kidney beans and add to the sweetcorn with the green (bell) pepper. Core and roughly chop the apple and add to the dish.
4 Prepare the dressing by putting the curry powder, orange juice, grated orange rind, olive oil and a little black pepper into a small bowl. Whisk with a fork to blend. Stir in the parsley.
5 Pour the dressing over the vegetables. Stir to coat.
6 Set aside for 10 minutes to let the flavours mingle, then serve.

Hot Mustardy New Potatoes

New potatoes are full of vitamin C and also contain plenty of fibre. Tossed in a mustardy French dressing whilst still warm, this dish is high on flavour and health.

PREPARATION TIME: *5 mins*   FREEZING: *Not suitable*
COOKING TIME: *7–15 mins*   SERVES: *4*

Imperial (Metric)	*American*
1 lb (450g) new potatoes	1 pound new potatoes

For the dressing

1 tablespoon wholegrain or French mustard	1 tablespoon wholegrain or French mustard
2 tablespoons olive oil	2 tablespoons olive oil
Juice of 1 lemon	Juice of 1 lemon
A little sea salt and freshly ground black pepper	A little sea salt and freshly ground black pepper

1 Scrub the potatoes clean and prick each one once with a fork. Cook, covered, in a pan of water, until just tender. Alternatively, put the pricked potatoes into a suitable bowl with 3 tablespoons water. Cover and microwave on 100% (full power) for 7 minutes. Allow to stand for 5 minutes.
2 Meanwhile, prepare the dressing. Put the mustard into a small bowl. Blend in the oil and lemon juice. Season to taste with the salt and pepper.
3 Drain the potatoes and transfer to a warm serving dish. Pour the dressing over and toss to coat. Either serve immediately or leave to cool.

Tomatoes Italian Style

This traditional Italian recipe makes a speedy, colourful starter or simple vegetable dish. Prepare the dressing in advance but don't add it until you are ready to serve. The fresh herbs are delicious with the tomatoes and bring out the flavour of the cheese. Serve with chunks of wholewheat bread.

PREPARATION TIME: *10 mins* FREEZING: *Not suitable*
COOKING TIME: — SERVES: *4*

Imperial (Metric)	American
3 large beefsteak tomatoes	3 large beefsteak tomatoes
5 oz (150g) Mozzarella cheese, thinly sliced	⅔ cup thinly sliced Mozzarella cheese

For the dressing

4 tablespoons olive oil	4 tablespoons olive oil
2 tablespoons red wine vinegar	2 tablespoons red wine vinegar
1 clove garlic, crushed	1 clove garlic, crushed
1 tablespoon freshly chopped oregano or parsley	1 tablespoon freshly chopped oregano or parsley
Freshly ground black pepper	Freshly ground black pepper

1 Slice the tomatoes. Lay the slices of tomato, interleaved with the sliced cheese, on 4 side plates.
2 Combine all the ingredients for the dressing in a small bowl and whisk.
3 Pour the dressing over the tomatoes and cheese and serve immediately.

Vegetable Mornay

This tasty supper dish is ideal for vegetarians. A tossed green salad and warm French bread will make it into a complete meal.

PREPARATION TIME: *10 mins*   FREEZING: *Not suitable*
COOKING TIME: *28 mins*   SERVES: 4

Imperial (Metric)	American
1 medium cauliflower, florets only	1 medium cauliflower, florets only
10 fl oz (300ml) water	1¼ cups water
4 oz (100g) frozen baby sweetcorn	1 cup frozen baby corn

For the sauce

1½ oz (40g) polyunsaturated margarine	3 tablespoons polyunsaturated margarine
1½ oz (40g) wholewheat flour	2 tablespoons wholewheat flour
Semi-skimmed milk (see method)	Low-fat milk (see method)
2 oz (50g) mushrooms, chopped	½ cup chopped mushrooms

For the topping

2 large slices wholewheat bread	2 large slices wholewheat bread
2 oz (50g) blue cheese, cheese	½ cup grated blue cheese
1 tablespoon sesame seeds	1 tablespoon sesame seeds

1 Preheat the oven to gas mark 6, 400°F (200°C).
2 Simmer the cauliflower florets in the water in a covered pan for 3 minutes. Add the corn, return the water to the boil and continue to simmer, covered, for a further 3 minutes, until the vegetables are just tender. Drain, reserving the liquid, and place the vegetables in a

shallow dish, halving each baby corn. Cover and keep warm.

3 Make the sauce: put the margarine and flour into a non-stick pan. Make the liquid reserved from the vegetables up to 1 pint (600ml/2½ cups) with milk and add to the pan. Stir continuously, using a balloon whisk, over a medium heat until the sauce boils and thickens. Stir the mushrooms into sauce. Pour the sauce over the vegetables to cover.

4 Cube the bread and sprinkle over evenly. Top with the cheese and sesame seeds.

5 Bake for 15 minutes near the top of the oven, then serve immediately.

Tomato, Crab and Celery Salad

This colourful salad is delicious on a buffet table or for a special lunch. Serve with wholewheat bread.

PREPARATION TIME: *10 mins* FREEZING: *Not suitable*
COOKING TIME: — SERVES: *4*

Imperial (Metric)	American
1 lb (450g) tomatoes	1 pound tomatoes
2 sticks celery	2 sticks celery
6 oz (175g) can crabmeat in brine, drained	6-ounce can crabmeat in brine, drained

For the dressing

4 tablespoons sunflower oil	4 tablespoons sunflower oil
2 tablespoons cider vinegar	2 tablespoons cider vinegar
1 teaspoon dried basil or 1 tablespoon freshly chopped	1 teaspoon dried basil or 1 tablespoon freshly chopped
1 clove garlic, crushed	1 clove garlic, crushed

1 Slice the tomatoes and finely chop the celery then arrange in a round shallow dish.
2 Flake the crab and distribute evenly over the vegetables.
3 Put all the ingredients for the dressing into a small bowl and whisk with a fork.
4 Pour the dressing over, set aside for 10 minutes for the flavours to mingle, then serve.

Glazed Courgette Ribbons with Beans

Courgette (zucchini) ribbons are prepared by simply topping and tailing the courgettes (zucchini), then making thin ribbons using a potato peeler, drawing it down the length of the courgette (zucchini). One courgette (zucchini) makes about 10 ribbons.

This vegetable dish makes a filling meal served on a bed of brown rice, topped with grated cheese.

PREPARATION TIME: *15 mins*   FREEZING: *Not suitable*
COOKING TIME: *8 mins*   SERVES: *4*

Imperial (Metric)	American
1 lb (450g) courgettes	1 pound zucchini
4 tablespoons sunflower oil	4 tablespoons sunflower oil
Grated rind of ½ orange	Grated rind of ½ orange
Juice of 1 orange	Juice of 1 orange
8 oz (225g) broad beans, fresh or frozen	2 cups fresh or frozen fava beans

To garnish
2 tablespoons freshly
chopped parsley

1 Make the courgettes (zucchini) into ribbons (see above).
2 Place the oil and the orange rind and juice in a large saucepan. Bring to the boil.
3 Add the broad (fava) beans and simmer, covered, for 5–6 minutes. Add the courgette (zucchini) ribbons and stir. Cover and simmer for 2 minutes.
4 Serve the vegetables with the liquid, sprinkled with the parsley.

Note: Carrot ribbons may be used as an alternative to the courgettes (zucchini).

Autumn Suppertime Eggs

Quickly cooked vegetables with eggs baked in the pan make a filling lunch or supper dish. Crusty French or wholewheat bread will make it into a complete meal.

PREPARATION TIME: *15 mins*   FREEZING: *Not suitable*
COOKING TIME: *20 mins*   SERVES: *4*

Imperial (Metric)	American
3 medium courgettes	3 medium zucchini
2 leeks	2 leeks
1 medium green pepper	1 medium green bell pepper
2 parsnips	2 parsnips
2 tablespoons sunflower oil	2 tablespoons sunflower oil
1 clove garlic, crushed	1 clove garlic, crushed
14 oz (400g) can chopped tomatoes with herbs	14-ounce can chopped tomatoes with herbs
A little sea salt and freshly ground black pepper	A little sea salt and freshly ground black pepper
4 eggs	4 eggs

1 Prepare the vegetables: slice the courgettes (zucchini) and clean and slice the leeks. Deseed and chop the (bell) pepper then peel and dice the parsnips.
2 Heat the oil in a large frying pan (skillet), then add the courgettes (zucchini) with the leeks, green pepper, parsnips and garlic.
3 Cook, stirring, over a medium heat for about 5 minutes, until the vegetables soften and start to brown.
4 Stir in the tomatoes. Season with salt and pepper.
5 Simmer, uncovered, for about 10 minutes, until the vegetables are tender and the liquid has reduced to a thick sauce.
6 Using the back of a tablespoon, make 4 slight indents in the vegetable mixture. One at a time, crack each egg into a cup and transfer to indent.
7 Cover with a lid and continue to cook gently until the eggs are set, approximately 3 minutes. Serve immediately with bread.

Brussels Sprout and Red Pepper Stir Fry

Nutty-tasting Brussels sprouts are part of the cabbage family and are full of vitamin C and fibre. This recipe is delicious around Christmas time and looks colourful on the festive table. It is also delicious with rice dishes.

PREPARATION TIME: *15 mins* FREEZING: *Not suitable*
COOKING TIME: *12 mins* SERVES: *4*

Imperial (Metric)	American
1 lb (450g) Brussels sprouts	1 pound Brussels sprouts
1 medium onion	1 medium onion
1 red pepper	1 red bell pepper
3 tablespoons olive oil	3 tablespoons olive oil
3 tablespoons pine kernels	3 tablespoons pine kernels
Rind and juice of ½ lemon	Rind and juice of ½ lemon
Freshly ground black pepper	Freshly ground black pepper

1 Bring a pan of water to the boil, put the sprouts into a steamer and steam them over the water for 5 minutes, turning them once or twice to ensure they cook evenly.
2 Peel and slice the onion. Deseed and chop the red (bell) pepper.
3 Heat the oil in a frying pan (skillet) and fry the onion and red (bell) pepper for about 4 minutes, then add the pine kernels. Stir these around until they are lightly browned.
4 Add the lemon rind and juice and the steamed sprouts.
5 Stir until thoroughly heated, season with black pepper and serve immediately.

ONE-POT COOKING

The recipes in this section provide main meals cooked in one pot – from 'Colourful Vegetable Risotto' to 'Vegetable Dhal' you will find dishes that are simple to prepare and easy on the washing-up too. Serving suggestions are given for all the recipes to help you to make a complete and filling meal fairly quickly.

Busy people may want to invest in an Automatic Cook Pot, also known as a Slow Cooker, which can be an absolute boon. These electric pots cook a family-sized meal while you get on with shopping, working or simply enjoying yourself. Make sure you buy one that is totally automatic and will switch from the higher 170 watts to the low 85 watts used in slow cooking, without your help. These clever work-top pots don't take up too much space and use about the same amount of power as a large light bulb.

For the Onion Bhajias in this section I have used a deep fat fryer. You may be surprised to find such a cooking method in a healthy cook book and I wouldn't suggest you deep fry frequently. This particular recipe uses healthy chick pea flour to make the bhajias which are quickly fried in oil. Treat this dish as 'a little bit of luxury' to serve as an occasional treat.

Vegetables in Spicy Peanut Sauce

Diced vegetables topped with a spicy sauce make a delicious lunch or supper which can be put together fast. Serve this high-fibre meal, which also provides protein, with brown rice or noodles.

PREPARATION TIME: *15 mins* FREEZING: *Suitable*
COOKING TIME: *23 mins* SERVES: *4*

Imperial (Metric)	American
1 medium onion	1 medium onion
1 medium cooking apple	1 medium cooking apple
2 tablespoons sunflower oil	2 tablespoons sunflower oil
1 clove garlic, crushed	1 clove garlic, crushed
3 tablespoons wholewheat flour	3 tablespoons wholewheat flour
1 tablespoon curry powder	1 tablespoon curry powder
3 tablespoons crunchy peanut butter	3 tablespoons crunchy peanut butter
1 pint (600ml) vegetable stock	2½ cups vegetable stock
1½ lb (675g) mixed vegetables, e.g. carrots, courgettes, mushrooms, parsnips	1½ pounds mixed vegetables, e.g. carrots, zucchini, mushrooms, parsnips

1 Peel and chop the onion and the apple.
2 Heat the oil in a large saucepan then sauté the onion and apple with the garlic for 3 minutes.
3 Stir in the flour with the curry powder. Cook for 2 minutes, stirring.
4 Blend the peanut butter with a little of the stock, then add to the pan with the remaining stock.
5 Bring to the boil, stirring. Simmer for 2–3 minutes.
6 Peel the vegetables and cut them into fairly large pieces.
7 Add the vegetables to the pot, cover and simmer for 15 minutes, until the vegetables are tender-crisp. Serve immediately.

Leek and Lentil Soup

Although green lentils do take about 50 minutes to cook, this soup can be left unattended after the initial preparation. Lentils are a valuable source of protein. They also supply carbohydrate, vitamin B, iron and calcium.

This filling soup is a meal in itself when served with bread and cheese or pâté – choose low-fat varieties if possible.

PREPARATION TIME: *10 mins*   FREEZING: *Suitable at end of stage 4*
COOKING TIME: *1 hour*   SERVES: *4–6*

Imperial (Metric)	American
2 leeks	2 leeks
2 tablespoons sunflower oil	2 tablespoons sunflower oil
6 oz (175g) green lentils	1 cup green lentils
1¾ pints (1 litre) vegetable stock	4½ cups vegetable stock
Freshly ground black pepper	Freshly ground black pepper
1 sachet bouquet garni	1 sachet bouquet garni
5 fl oz (150ml) plain yoghurt	⅔ cup plain yoghurt
2 oz (50g) reduced-fat Cheddar cheese, grated	½ cup grated reduced-fat Cheddar cheese

1 Clean and slice the leeks, then heat the oil in a large saucepan and sauté them for about 5 minutes, until they begin to soften.
2 Wash the lentils in a sieve then add them to the pan with the vegetable stock. Season with black pepper and add the bouquet garni.
3 Bring to the boil, cover and simmer for approximately 50 minutes, until the lentils are soft.
4 Turn into a food processor and process until smooth. Return to the pan.
5 Stir in the yoghurt and heat through without boiling.
6 Serve immediately, sprinkled with the grated cheese.
Note: For a change replace 5 fl oz (150ml/⅔ cup) of the stock with white wine or cider.

Clockwise from top left:

1 Oriental Microwave Chicken
2 Onion Bhajias
3 Creamy Curried Halibut

4 Rainbow Pepper Salad with Mackerel
5 Bulgar Wheat Savoury
6 Chicken, Rice and Beansprout Stir Fry
7 Leek and Lentil Soup

Clockwise from top left:

1 Raspberry and Blackcurrant
  Compote with Yoghurt
2 Fruity Granola

3 Speedy Cheese and Onion Flan
4 Garlicky Aubergine Pâté
5 Tomato and Herb Gratin
6 Peking Stir Fry
7 Stuffed Mushrooms

Clockwise from top left:

1 Apple Sponge
2 Lemon Whip with Plums
3 Macaroni au Gratin Special

4 Glazed Courgette Ribbons with Beans
5 Florida Cocktail
6 Apricot Slices
7 Vegetable Stroganoff
8 Green Pasta with Baby Corn

Clockwise from top:

1 Speedy Paella
2 Celery and Herb Bread
3 Avocado Dip

4 Vegetarian Pasta Supper
5 Fruit Juice Set Dessert with Fresh Fruits
6 Creamy Layered Apricot Crunch
7 Lemon Sorbet

Clockwise from top:

1 Brussel Sprout and Red Pepper Stir Fry
2 Brown Rice Pilaff
3 Red Kidney Bean and Cashew Hotpot

4 Orange and Walnut Salad
5 Curried Chicken Toasted Sandwiches
6 Easy Wholewheat Pizza
7 Easy Peach Ice-Cream
8 Chicken with Wine and Red Grapes

Clockwise from top left:

1 Avocado and Green Fruit Salad
2 Garlic and Cheddar Lettuce Cups
3 Chicken Liver and Mushroom Salad

4 Tomato and Apple Soup
5 Chive and Blue Cheese Dip
6 Avocado with Light Herb Cheese
7 Pink Salmon and Mushroom Pâté
8 Tomatoes Italian Style

Clockwise from top:

1 Royal Salad
2 Bulgar Wheat and Almond Salad
3 Vegetable Mornay

4 Easy Cheesey Tomatoes
5 Sunshine Soup
6 Curried Kidney Bean and Corn Salad
7 Anchovy-Stuffed Eggs
8 Carrot Cake with Lemon Top

Clockwise from top left:

1 Ratatouille
2 Poppyseed Pudding with Apricot
   Sauce
3 Caribbean Salad
4 Quick Turkey Curry
5 Tomato, Crab and Celery Salad
6 Pasta and Olive Salad
7 Quick Pizzas

Peking Stir Fry

Speedy, nutritious and fun, that's stir fry. Serve this Oriental dish with rice or noodles for a delicious, high-fibre dinner party.

PREPARATION TIME: *15 mins*   FREEZING: *Not suitable*
COOKING TIME: *9 mins*   SERVES: *4*

Imperial (Metric)	American
1 onion	1 onion
½ Savoy cabbage	½ Savoy cabbage
2 medium carrots	2 medium carrots
3 oz (75g) mangetout	½ cup snow peas
2 tablespoons olive oil	2 tablespoons olive oil
8 oz (225g) peeled prawns	1 cup peeled shrimps
5 oz (150g) jar yellow bean sauce	5-ounce jar yellow bean sauce

1 Prepare the vegetables: peel and thinly slice the onion and finely shred the cabbage. Scrub clean the carrots and cut them into matchsticks, then trim the mangetout (snow peas) and slice them at an angle.
2 Heat the oil in a wok or large frying pan (skillet). Stir fry the onion and cabbage for 3 minutes.
3 Add the mangetout (snow peas) and carrots. Stir fry for a further 2 minutes.
4 Lower the heat and add the prawns (shrimps) and yellow bean sauce. Heat through thoroughly, stirring.
5 Serve immediately with rice or noodles.

Piperade

Eggs are a valuable source of protein, vitamins and minerals although there is cholesterol in the yolk, so it's best to restrict yourself to no more than four a week. Piperade is a mixture of scrambled eggs and vegetables cooked together in one pan, resulting in a filling lunch or supper dish which is delicious with wholewheat toast.

PREPARATION TIME: *10 mins*   FREEZING: *Not suitable*
COOKING TIME: *10 mins*   SERVES: *4*

Imperial (Metric)	American
4 spring onions	4 scallions
½ red pepper	½ red (bell) pepper
2 courgettes	2 zucchini
2 tablespoons olive oil	2 tablespoons olive oil
4 oz (100g) button mushrooms, chopped	1 cup chopped button mushrooms
8 eggs	8 eggs
6 tablespoons semi-skimmed milk	6 tablespoons low-fat milk
A little sea salt and freshly ground black pepper	A little sea salt and freshly ground black pepper

To serve
Wholewheat toast and
grated Parmesan cheese

1 Chop the spring onions (scallions). Deseed and chop the red (bell) pepper, then slice the courgettes (zucchini).
2 Heat the oil in a medium-sized non-stick saucepan then gently sauté the spring onions (scallions) and red (bell) pepper for 2 minutes.
3 Add the courgettes (zucchini) and mushrooms and continue to sauté for a further 3–4 minutes.
4 Meanwhile beat together the eggs and milk and season lightly.

5 Pour the egg mixture into the pan and cook gently,
  stirring, until just scrambled.
6 Pile on to hot toast and serve immediately, sprinkled
  with Parmesan cheese.

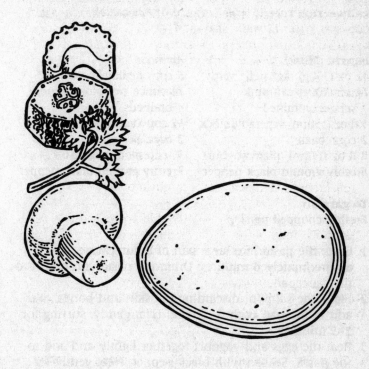

Creamy Pasta with Salmon

Tagliatelle verdi is coils of pasta, lightly flavoured with spinach. In this simple recipe it is served with a sauce made of canned pink salmon, which is high in protein, calcium and vitamins A and D, and plain yoghurt.

PREPARATION TIME: *5 mins*   FREEZING: *Not suitable*
COOKING TIME: *12 mins*   SERVES: *4*

Imperial (Metric)	*American*
12 oz (350g) tagliatelle verdi	6 cups tagliatelle verdi
14 oz (400g) can pink salmon, drained	14-ounce can pink salmon, drained
5 fl oz (150ml) vegetable stock	⅔ cup vegetable stock
2 eggs, beaten	2 eggs, beaten
5 fl oz (150ml) plain yoghurt	⅔ cup plain yoghurt
Freshly ground black pepper	Freshly ground black pepper

To garnish
Freshly chopped parsley

1 Cook the pasta in a large pan of boiling water for approximately 6 minutes. Drain the pasta and return to the saucepan.
2 Flake the salmon, discarding the skin and bones, and add to the pan with the stock. Heat gently, stirring for 2–3 minutes.
3 Beat the eggs and yoghurt together lightly and add to the pasta. Season with black pepper. Heat gently for 2–3 minutes, stirring.
4 Serve immediately, sprinkled with the parsley.

Onion Bhajias

These Indian savouries are quick to cook and delicious served either as a starter or main meal when accompanied by a salad and naan bread. Use vegetable oil for deep frying and ensure that the oil is heated to the correct temperature before immersing the food, that way the food is cooked quickly, with the flavour locked in and the minimum amount of oil absorbed by the food.

Gram (chick pea) flour is readily available from Asian stores and some health food shops.

PREPARATION TIME: *15 mins*   FREEZING: *Not suitable*
COOKING TIME: *15 mins*   MAKES: *12 bhajias*

Imperial (Metric)	*American*
Sunflower oil for deep frying	Sunflower oil for deep frying
2 medium onions	2 medium onions
9 rounded tablespoons gram (chick pea) flour	9 rounded tablespoons gram (chick pea) flour
½ teaspoon salt	½ teaspoon salt
1 teaspoon turmeric	1 teaspoon turmeric
2 teaspoons garam masala	2 teaspoons garam masala
1 teaspoon dried parsley or 1 tablespoon freshly chopped	1 teaspoon dried parsley or 1 tablespoon freshly chopped
1 teaspoon ground cumin	1 teaspoon ground cumin
4 fl oz (120ml) cold water	½ cup cold water

To serve
Freshly chopped coriander
  (optional)

1 Heat the oil to 180°C/350°F in a deep frying pan (skillet).
2 Peel and thinly slice the onions.
3 Pour the flour into a large mixing bowl and stir in the salt, turmeric, garam masala, parsley and cumin.
4 Gradually add the water, mixing to form a smooth, thick batter. Stir in the onion slices.

5 Push dessertspoons of the mixture into the pan of hot oil. Fry 3 at a time for 4–5 minutes, until golden.
6 Drain on absorbent kitchen paper and serve sprinkled with the coriander, if using.

Speedy Cheese and Onion Flan

Try this reduced-fat frozen pastry next time you want to make a quiche in a hurry. It's made with a reduced amount of polyunsaturated fat, is crisp and delicious.

You will need a 7 in (17.5cm) loose-bottomed flan tin.

PREPARATION TIME: *10 mins + chill time*   FREEZING: *Suitable*
COOKING TIME: *35 mins*   SERVES: *4*

Imperial (Metric)	*American*
6 oz (175g) Jus Roll reduced-fat frozen puff pastry, defrosted	6 ounces reduced-fat frozen puff pastry, defrosted
3 spring onions	3 scallions
1 tablespoon freshly chopped parsley	1 tablespoon freshly chopped parsley
3 eggs	3 eggs
10 fl oz (300ml) semi-skimmed milk	1¼ cups low-fat milk
A little sea salt and freshly ground black pepper	A little sea salt and freshly ground black pepper
3 oz (75g) reduced-fat Cheddar cheese, grated	¾ cup grated reduced-fat Cheddar cheese

1 Preheat the oven to gas mark 6, 400°F (200°C).
2 Roll the pastry out evenly and use to line the flan tin. Roll across the top of the tin to neaten the edges. Chill for 20 minutes.
3 Bake the pastry case blind by lining with a piece of scrunched up kitchen foil, for 10 minutes, until dry.
4 Finely chop the spring onions (scallions) and sprinkle evenly over the base of the flan. Add the parsley.
5 Beat together the eggs and milk. Season lightly with the sea salt and pepper. Pour into the flan case. Sprinkle over the cheese.
6 Return the flan to the oven. Reduce the temperature to gas mark 5, 375°F (190°C) and bake for a further 20–25 minutes, until golden.
7 Serve immediately or allow to cool and serve cold.

Bulgur Wheat Savoury

Bulgur, or cracked wheat, is quick and simple to use and tastes delicious; it's filling and nutritious too. Try this well-flavoured recipe for a quick lunch or supper. Serve with a green salad and bread.

PREPARATION TIME: *15 mins*   FREEZING: *Not suitable*
COOKING TIME: *30 mins*   SERVES: *4–6*

Imperial (Metric)	American
8 oz (225g) bulgur wheat	2 cups bulgur wheat
15 fl oz (450ml) boiling water	2 cups boiling water
½ young leek	½ young leek
14 oz (400g) can chopped tomatoes	14-ounce can chopped tomatoes
1 tablespoon freshly chopped chervil	1 tablespoon freshly chopped chervil
A little sea salt and cayenne pepper	A little sea salt and cayenne pepper
1 clove garlic, crushed	1 clove garlic, crushed
2 tablespoons lemon juice	2 tablespoons lemon juice
2 hardboiled eggs	2 hardcooked eggs
3 tablespoons grated Parmesan cheese	3 tablespoons grated Parmesan cheese
½ medium cucumber	½ medium cucumber
2 oz (50g) chopped walnuts	½ cup chopped walnuts

To garnish
Wedges of lemon

1 Put the bulgur wheat into a large mixing bowl and pour over the boiling water. Leave to stand for 30 minutes, until cool.
2 Fluff the bulgur up with a fork. Slice the leek finely and add to the bowl. Add the tomatoes, chervil, a seasoning of sea salt and cayenne pepper, the garlic and lemon juice. Refrigerate for 1–2 hours.
3 Chop the eggs and fork into the salad with the

Parmesan cheese. Chop the cucumber and add.
4 Serve immediately, sprinkled with the chopped
  walnuts and garnished with the wedges of lemon.

Spanish Omelette

Omelettes are quick to prepare and cook, and they're filling and tasty too. Eggs are a valuable source of protein, vitamins and minerals and although egg yolks do contain cholesterol, it is now considered fine to include them in a healthy diet in moderation.

PREPARATION TIME: *10 mins*   FREEZING: *Not suitable*
COOKING TIME: *30 mins*   SERVES: *4*

Imperial (Metric)	American
2 medium onions	2 medium onions
1 red pepper	1 red bell pepper
2 large potatoes	2 large potatoes
3 tablespoons sunflower oil	3 tablespoons sunflower oil
2 cloves garlic, crushed	2 cloves garlic, crushed
2 tomatoes	2 tomatoes
6 eggs	6 eggs
A little sea salt and freshly ground black pepper	A little sea salt and freshly ground black pepper

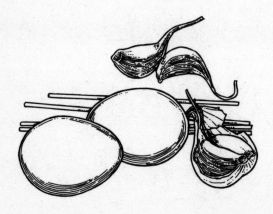

1 Peel and chop the onions. Deseed and chop the red (bell) pepper.
2 Dice the potatoes and boil them until tender (5–7 minutes), then drain.
3 Heat 2 tablespoons of the oil in a large frying pan (skillet). Add the onions and sauté for 5–7 minutes until softened and starting to brown. Add the garlic, potatoes and red (bell) pepper. Chop the tomatoes and add to the pan. Cook over a medium heat, stirring occasionally, for a further 5 minutes.
4 In a large bowl whisk the eggs with a little seasoning and 4 tablespoons cold water. Stir the sautéed vegetables into the beaten eggs.
5 Heat the remaining oil in the pan, pour in the egg mixture, and cook for about 8 minutes over a medium heat until the omelette loosens from the edge of the pan and is almost set.
6 Sprinkle the cheese over the top and place under a preheated grill (broiler) to finish cooking the top of the omelette. Serve.

Braised Vegetables with Tofu

A colourful vegetable stew with added protein, which makes a tasty lunch or supper dish.

This filling dish is excellent served with wholewheat bread.

PREPARATION TIME: *15 mins*   FREEZING: *Not suitable*
COOKING TIME: *38 mins*   SERVES: *4*

Imperial (Metric)	American
2 tablespoons sunflower oil	2 tablespoons sunflower oil
12 oz (350g) bean curd	1½ cups bean curd
1 medium aubergine	1 medium eggplant
4 sticks celery	4 sticks celery
½ large swede	½ large rutabaga
2 large carrots	2 large carrots
1 teaspoon dried basil or 1 tablespoon freshly chopped	1 teaspoon dried basil or 1 tablespoon freshly chopped
2 bay leaves	2 bay leaves
2 tablespoons tomato paste	2 tablespoons tomato paste
15 fl oz (450ml) vegetable stock	2 cups vegetable stock
1 tablespoon wholewheat flour	1 tablespoon wholewheat flour

1 Heat the oil in a large saucepan. Cube the bean curd and add to the pan; sauté on all sides, until lightly browned. Remove the pan from the heat and drain the bean curd on kitchen paper.
2 Dice the aubergine (eggplant), chop the celery and peel and dice the swede (rutabaga). Scrub the carrots clean and dice them.
3 Reheat the oil left in the pan. Sauté the aubergine (eggplant), celery, swede (rutabaga) and carrots for about 7 minutes.
4 Add the basil, bay leaves and tomato paste. Pour on the stock, stirring.

5 Bring to the boil and simmer for about 30 minutes,
  until the vegetables are tender.
6 Blend the flour to a smooth paste with 2 tablespoons
  water and add to the pan. Simmer for 2 minutes,
  stirring. Stir in the tofu and reheat for 1–2 minutes,
  then serve.

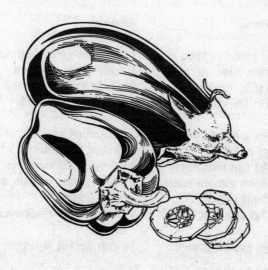

Black-Eyed Bean and Seafood Casserole

A lunch or supper dish that can be put together speedily from freezer and store-cupboard ingredients. Black-eyed beans are an excellent source of fibre, protein and carbohydrate. They contain approximately 95 calories per 4 oz (100g/1 cup). Cod is low in fat and also provides protein. Serve with brown rice or bread and a salad.

PREPARATION TIME: *10 mins*   FREEZING: *Not suitable*
COOKING TIME: *16 mins*   SERVES: *4*

Imperial (Metric)	American
2 leeks	2 leeks
1 medium green pepper	1 medium green bell pepper
1 tablespoon olive oil	1 tablespoon olive oil
2 cloves garlic, crushed	2 cloves garlic, crushed
½ teaspoon hot chilli powder	½ teaspoon hot chile powder
2 teaspoons ground coriander	2 teaspoons ground coriander
1 lb (450g) cod fillet	1 pound cod fillet
14oz (400g) can tomatoes	14-ounce can tomatoes
2 tablespoons tomato paste	2 tablespoons tomato paste
3 fl oz (85ml) water	⅓ cup water
15 oz (425g) can black-eyed beans	15-ounce can black-eyed beans
4 oz (100g) peeled prawns	½ cup peeled shrimps

To garnish
Freshly chopped parsley

1 Clean and slice the leeks. Deseed and roughly chop the green (bell) pepper.
2 Heat the oil in a large saucepan and gently sauté the leeks and garlic for about 5 minutes. Add the green pepper with the chilli (chile) powder and coriander. Cook, stirring, for a further minute.
3 Cut the cod into fairly large pieces and add to the pan

with the tomatoes and their juice, tomato paste and water.

4 Drain and rinse the beans and stir them gently into the pan.

5 Bring the stew to simmering point. Cover and cook gently for 8 minutes, or until the fish is cooked. Add the prawns (shrimps), stir and heat through gently.

6 Serve immediately, sprinkled with the parsley.

Chicken with Wine and Red Grapes

In this dish, high-protein, low-fat chicken is cooked in red wine then served with grapes. Adding beans to the dish before serving means there is no need to serve potatoes as an accompaniment, but warm wholewheat French sticks would be ideal to mop up the juices of this well-flavoured dish, and a tossed mixed salad would add colour, fibre and vitamins.

PREPARATION TIME: *10 mins*   FREEZING: *Not suitable*
COOKING TIME: *1 hour*   SERVES: *4*

Imperial (Metric)	American
2 onions	2 onions
1 chicken, skinned and divided into 8 portions	1 chicken, skinned and divided into 8 portions
2 tablespoons wholewheat flour	2 tablespoons wholewheat flour
2 cloves garlic, crushed	2 cloves garlic, crushed
2 tablespoons olive oil	2 tablespoons olive oil
15 fl oz (450ml) light red wine	2 cups light red wine
5 fl oz (150ml) chicken stock	⅔ cup chicken stock
1 tablespoon freshly chopped parsley	1 tablespoon freshly chopped parsley
15 oz (425g) can haricot beans, drained	15-ounce can haricot beans, drained
8 oz (225g) red seedless grapes	1⅓ cups red seedless grapes

To garnish
Freshly chopped parsley

1 Peel and chop the onions. Heat the oil in a large flameproof saucepan.
2 Toss the chicken pieces in the flour and fry in the heated oil, 4 pieces at a time, until browned. Transfer to a plate.
3 Sauté the onions and garlic in the pan for about

5 minutes, until the onions soften.

4 Return the chicken to the pan, pour over the wine and stock and add the parsley.

5 Bring to the boil, cover and simmer for 45 minutes, until the chicken is tender. Transfer the chicken to a serving dish, cover and keep warm.

6 Boil the liquid rapidly to reduce a little then rinse the beans and add to the pan with the grapes. Reheat gently, without boiling.

7 Spoon the sauce over the chicken and serve immediately, sprinkled with the chopped parsley.

Colourful Vegetable Risotto

This recipe uses flat mushrooms for their excellent flavour, with peas to add vitamin C, protein and carbohydrate and brown rice for carbohydrate, fibre and vitamin B.

PREPARATION TIME: *10 mins*   FREEZING: *Suitable at end of stage 4*
COOKING TIME: *45 mins*   SERVES: *6–8*

Imperial (Metric)	American
1 red-skinned onion	1 red-skinned onion
1 clove garlic	1 clove garlic
3 tablespoons olive oil	3 tablespoons olive oil
12 oz (350g) flat mushrooms, sliced	5½ cups sliced flat mushrooms
1 lb (450g) easy-cook brown rice	1 pound easy-cook brown rice
2½ pints (1.5 litres) vegetable stock, boiling	6¼ cups boiling vegetable stock
6 oz (175g) frozen peas	1½ cups frozen peas
4 oz (100g) frozen sweetcorn	1 cup frozen corn kernels
2 tablespoons freshly chopped parsley	2 tablespoons freshly chopped parsley
4 tablespoons grated Parmesan cheese (optional)	4 tablespoons grated Parmesan cheese (optional)

1 Peel and chop the onion and garlic.
2 Heat the oil in a large pan and sauté the onion and garlic for about 5 minutes, until softened.
3 Add the mushrooms and rice and stir gently for 2 minutes.
4 Slowly add 10 fl oz (300ml/1¼ cups) of the boiling stock. Simmer gently, uncovered, until absorbed. Add the remaining stock. Cover the pan and simmer for 30 minutes.
5 Stir in the peas, sweetcorn and parsley. Cover and simmer for a further 5 minutes. Serve immediately, sprinkled with Parmesan cheese if using.

Brown Rice Pilaff

This well-flavoured Indian-style vegetarian pilaff would make a good supper dish. Serve with a tomato and onion salad, naan bread and, if you have time to make it, Vegetable Dhal (page 108).

PREPARATION TIME: *10 mins*   FREEZING: *Suitable*
COOKING TIME: *35 mins*   SERVES: *4*

Imperial (Metric)	American
2 large leeks	2 large leeks
1 green pepper	1 green bell pepper
2 carrots	2 carrots
2 tablespoons olive oil	2 tablespoons olive oil
1 teaspoon garam masala	1 teaspoon garam masala
1 teaspoon turmeric	1 teaspoon turmeric
1 clove garlic, crushed	1 clove garlic, crushed
Pinch of chilli powder	Pinch of chile powder
10 oz (275g) easy cook brown rice	1⅛ cup easy-cook brown rice
1¼ pint (750ml) vegetable stock	3 cups vegetable stock
2 oz (50g) sultanas	½ cup golden seedless raisins

1 Clean and slice the leeks and deseed and chop the green (bell) pepper. Scrub clean and dice the carrots.
2 Heat the oil in a medium saucepan. Stir in the garam masala, turmeric, garlic and chilli (chile) powder. Cook over a medium heat for 1 minute.
3 Add the vegetables and fry, stirring, for 5 minutes.
4 Add the rice and stock to the pan with the sultanas (golden seedless raisins). Cover and cook gently for 20–25 minutes, until the rice is tender and most of the liquid has been absorbed.
5 Leave the pan covered, off the heat, for 5 minutes before serving.

Vegetable Dhal

This high-fibre dhal makes a delicious meal on its own, served with hardboiled (hardcooked) eggs. Alternatively serve it as part of an Indian dinner party, with Brown Rice Pilaff (page 107) and a leaf salad.

PREPARATION TIME: *10 mins*   FREEZING: *Not suitable*
COOKING TIME: *44 mins*   SERVES: *4*

Imperial (Metric)	American
2 medium onions	2 medium onions
1 small aubergine	1 small eggplant
2 tablespoons olive oil	2 tablespoons olive oil
1 clove garlic, crushed	1 clove garlic, crushed
1 teaspoon turmeric	1 teaspoon turmeric
½ teaspoon ground cumin	½ teaspoon ground cumin
4 oz (100g) split red lentils, rinsed	¾ cup rinsed split red lentils
Juice of ½ lime	Juice of ½ lime
1 teaspoon ground coriander	1 teaspoon ground coriander
1¼ pints (750ml) vegetable stock	3 cups vegetable stock
11 oz (300g) can new potatoes, drained	11-ounce can new potatoes, drained
2 teaspoons garam masala	2 teaspoons garam masala

1 Peel and slice the onions and dice the aubergine (eggplant).
2 Heat the oil in a medium-sized saucepan. Add the onions, garlic, turmeric and cumin. Stir-fry gently for 1 minute.
3 Stir in the aubergine (eggplant), lentils, lime juice and coriander with the stock. Bring to the boil. Cover and simmer for 30 minutes, then remove the lid and boil rapidly for 10 minutes to reduce the liquid.
4 Drain the potatoes and add to the pan with the garam masala. Stir over a gentle heat until thoroughly hot. Serve immediately.

Chicken, Rice and Beansprout Stir Fry

Chicken is cooked quickly with beansprouts and baby corn to preserve all the nutrients and make a colourful, high-fibre, low-fat meal.

PREPARATION TIME: *10 mins*   FREEZING: *Not suitable*
COOKING TIME: *10 mins*   SERVES: *4*

Imperial (Metric)	*American*
1 lb (450g) skinned and boned chicken breast	1 pound skinned and boned chicken breast
2 tablespoons sunflower oil	2 tablespoons sunflower oil
6 oz (175g) beansprouts	3 cups beansprouts
6 oz (175g) frozen baby sweetcorn	1½ cups frozen baby corn
1 clove garlic, crushed	1 clove garlic, crushed
1 teaspoon arrowroot	1 teaspoon arrowroot
5 fl oz (150ml) apple juice	⅔ cup apple juice
10 oz (275g) frozen pre-cooked long grain brown rice	5 cups frozen pre-cooked long grain brown rice
A little sea salt and freshly ground black pepper	A little sea salt and freshly ground black pepper

To garnish
2 tablespoons freshly chopped parsley

1 Slice the chicken breast thinly into strips.
2 Heat the oil in a wok or large frying pan (skillet). Stir fry the chicken over a high heat for approximately 3 minutes.
3 Add the beansprouts, baby corn and garlic. Continue to stir-fry for 3 minutes.
4 Blend the arrowroot and apple juice together. Add to the pan with the rice. Season with salt and pepper.
5 Bring to the boil, stirring. Cover and simmer for 2 minutes then serve sprinkled with the parsley.

Creamy Curried Halibut

Fish is one of the quickest protein foods to cook, and it's easy to digest too.

Serve this spicy, mild curry with brown rice and sliced bananas sprinkled with lemon juice.

PREPARATION TIME: *10 mins*   FREEZING: *Suitable*
COOKING TIME: *10 mins*   SERVES: *4*

Imperial (Metric)	American
2 leeks	2 leeks
2 tablespoons sunflower oil	2 tablespoons sunflower oil
1 clove garlic, crushed	1 clove garlic, crushed
1 teaspoon turmeric powder	1 teaspoon turmeric powder
1 teaspoon curry powder	1 teaspoon curry powder
1 teaspoon dried oregano or 1 tablespoon freshly chopped	1 teaspoon dried oregano or 1 tablespoon freshly chopped
2 rounded tablespoons wholewheat flour	2 rounded tablespoons wholewheat flour
14 oz (400g) can reduced-fat evaporated milk	14-ounce can reduced-fat evaporated milk
5 fl oz (150ml) fish or chicken stock	⅔ cup fish or chicken stock
2 teaspoons lime juice	2 teaspoons lime juice
1½ lb (675g) halibut fillet, cubed	1½ pounds cubed halibut fillet

1 Clean and slice the leeks.
2 Heat the oil in a large saucepan. Sauté the leeks, garlic, turmeric, curry powder and oregano for 2 minutes. Add the flour and cook, stirring, for a further 2 minutes.
3 Gradually add the milk and the stock.
4 Heat, stirring constantly, until the mixture boils and thickens. Add the lime juice and halibut.
5 Cover and cook over a very gentle heat for 5–7 minutes, until the fish is cooked. Serve immediately.

CALORIE-COUNTED MEALS

Don't despair if you're managing to follow a calorie-controlled diet during the week only to find it difficult to entertain guests at the weekend without serving calorie-laden goodies.

This chapter offers eight menus, each consisting of a main course and a dessert, which have been carefully calorie counted so that you can impress your guests and enjoy your dinner party without increasing your waistline!

Serving suggestions for side dishes should be followed, as it's surprising how quickly you can add a vast amount of calories to a simple salad, for example, by using a rich dressing.

Alcohol is full of empty calories, so restrict your intake to one or at the most two glasses of wine. Try having half a glass of wine, either white or red, topped up with soda water for a long refreshing drink which will last a long time.

If you like to serve a starter, restrict it to fresh fruits – try melon served with a raspberry coulis made by sieving about 8 oz (225g/2 cups) raspberries and adding just 1 teaspoon raw cane sugar to the resulting purée; this will give enough coulis for 4 people. Pink grapefruit is delicious cold, or try it hot – just heat under the grill (broiler), sprinkled with a little ground cinnamon or ginger.

MENU 1
Broccoli and Leek Roulade

This vegetarian dish is quick to prepare and cook, yet looks most impressive for a special occasion. Serve warm with French bread and a mixed salad.

PREPARATION TIME: *15 mins*   FREEZING: *Not suitable*
COOKING TIME: *30 mins*   SERVES: *4*
KCALS PER SERVING: *about 354*

Imperial (Metric)	American
12 oz (350g) fresh broccoli spears	3 cups fresh broccoli spears
1 medium leek	1 medium leek
1 oz (25g) polyunsaturated margarine	2 tablespoons polyunsaturated margarine
4 eggs	4 eggs
A little sea salt and freshly ground black pepper	A little sea salt and freshly ground black pepper
2 tablespoons grated Parmesan cheese	2 tablespoons grated Parmesan cheese

For the filling

1 tablespoon sunflower oil	1 tablespoon sunflower oil
6 oz (175g) mushrooms, sliced	1½ cups sliced mushrooms
1 tablespoon wholewheat flour	1 tablespoon wholewheat flour
10 fl oz (300ml) semi-skimmed milk	1¼ cups low-fat milk
2 oz (50g) reduced-fat Cheddar cheese, grated	½ cup grated reduced-fat Cheddar cheese

1   Preheat the oven to gas mark 6, 200°F (400°F). Grease and line a 12in × 8in (30cm × 20cm) Swiss roll (jelly roll) tin.
2   Finely chop the broccoli and the leek.

3 Melt the margarine in a medium-sized saucepan. Sauté the broccoli and the leek for 7–8 minutes, until softened.

4 Transfer to a large mixing bowl. Separate the eggs and add the yolks to the broccoli and leeks. Season lightly with salt and pepper.

5 Whisk the egg whites in a clean bowl until fairly stiff. Stir 2 tablespoons of the egg white into the broccoli mixture to lighten it, then carefully but quickly fold in the remainder.

6 Turn the mixture into the prepared tin and level the surface. Bake for 10–15 minutes, until risen and firm.

7 Meanwhile, prepare the filling. Heat the oil in a medium-sized pan. Add the mushrooms and sauté for about 3 minutes. Add the flour and stir over a low heat for 1 minute. Gradually add the milk.

8 Bring to the boil, stirring, then simmer for 1–2 minutes, stirring, until the sauce thickens. Remove from the heat and stir in the cheese to melt.

9 Sprinkle the Parmesan cheese on to a sheet of greaseproof paper (baking parchment). Turn the roulade out on to the cheese and peel away the lining paper.

10 Spread evenly with the sauce to within ½in (1cm) of the sides.

11 Roll up and serve immediately.

Creamy Lime Cheese with Strawberries

This creamy dessert with the added luxury of fresh strawberries is a delicious way to round off almost any meal. Curd cheese provides calcium and protein, as does the fromage frais. Strawberries add vitamin C and fibre. Use other fresh fruits, such as plums, mango, grapes or peaches, when strawberries are not in season. The rind and juice of half an orange could be substituted for the lime juice.

PREPARATION TIME: *15 mins + chill time*   FREEZING: *Not suitable*
COOKING TIME: —   SERVES: *4*
KCALS PER SERVING: *about 137*

Imperial (Metric)	*American*
6 oz (175g) curd cheese	1½ cups pot cheese
8 tablespoons low-fat fromage frais	8 tablespoons low-fat fromage frais
Rind and juice of 1 lime	Rind and juice of 1 lime
3 tablespoons clear honey	3 tablespoons clear honey
8 oz (225g) fresh strawberries, sliced	2 cups sliced fresh strawberries
2 egg whites	2 egg whites

1 Turn the curd (pot) cheese into a mixing bowl and beat in the fromage frais with the lime rind and juice and the honey. Fold in the sliced strawberries, reserving a few slices for decoration.
2 Whisk the egg whites until stiff then fold them into the cheese mixture.
3 Pile into 4 wine glasses and refrigerate for 30 minutes.
4 Serve decorated with the reserved strawberries.

MENU 2
Bulgur Wheat and Almond Salad

Bulgur wheat is a valuable source of carbohydrate and also provides some protein and vitamin B.

PREPARATION TIME: *15 mins*   FREEZING: *Not suitable*
COOKING TIME: —   SERVES: *4*
KCALS PER SERVING: *about 245*

Imperial (Metric)	American
8 oz (225g) bulgur wheat	2 cups bulgur wheat
15 fl oz (450ml) boiling water	2 cups boiling water
2 cloves garlic, crushed	2 cloves garlic, crushed
1 small green pepper	1 small green pepper
3 spring onions	3 scallions
1 small pineapple	1 small pineapple
3 tablespoons freshly chopped parsley	3 tablespoons freshly chopped parsley
3 tablespoons light soy sauce	3 tablespoons light soy sauce
Grated rind and juice of 2 lemons	Grated rind and juice of 2 lemons
3 tablespoons olive oil	3 tablespoons olive oil
Freshly ground black pepper	Freshly ground black pepper
2 oz (50g) toasted almonds	½ cup toasted almonds

To serve
Mixed salad leaves

1 Put the bulgur wheat into a mixing bowl and pour the boiling water over it. Fork through from time to time and set aside until cold. (It can be prepared the day before and stored in the refrigerator overnight, if preferred.)

2 Fluff up the bulgur wheat with a fork, add the garlic, then deseed and chop the green pepper, chop the spring onions (scallions), peel, core and chop the pineapple, and add to the bulgur with the parsley and

the soy sauce. Add the lemon rind and juice, mix well, then pour over the oil and season with the black pepper. Toss again to coat.

3 Arrange the salad leaves on a large plate and turn the bulgur salad into the centre.

4 Serve immediately, sprinkled with the almonds.

Spiced Bananas

Bananas taste totally different hot and they're high on fibre, so enjoy this luxurious-tasting sweet and don't feel guilty afterwards – the calorie count isn't so high after all.

PREPARATION TIME: *10 mins*   FREEZING: *Not suitable*
COOKING TIME: *4 mins*   SERVES: *4*
KCALS PER SERVING: *about 115*

Imperial (Metric)
4 medium bananas
4 teaspoons raw cane sugar
2 teaspoons ground ginger
4 tablespoons pure orange
  juice

American
4 medium bananas
4 teaspoons raw cane sugar
2 teaspoons ground ginger
4 tablespoons pure orange
  juice

To serve
4 tablespoons low-fat
  fromage frais

1 Line the grill (broiler) rack with foil and preheat to medium hot.
2 Peel and halve the bananas lengthways and lay them, cut side up, on the foil.
3 Mix together the sugar and ginger, then divide evenly between the bananas, sprinkling it over.
4 Pour 1 tablespoon of orange juice over each banana.
5 Grill (broil) until hot and bubbling – about 3–4 minutes.
6 Lift the bananas on to a serving plate, then carefully lift the foil and pour the juices over the bananas. Serve warm with the fromage frais.

MENU 3
Quick Turkey Curry

This fairly mild curry is a delicious way of using up turkey, but you could use chicken or Quorn instead. The curry has a fruity theme, supplying plenty of colour and fibre, and is delicious served with brown rice, or with pitta bread and salad if you are in a real rush.

PREPARATION TIME: *15 mins*   FREEZING: *Not suitable*
COOKING TIME: *30 mins*   SERVES: *4*
KCALS PER SERVING: *about 340*

Imperial (Metric)	*American*
1 medium onion	1 medium onion
2 tablespoons sunflower oil	2 tablespoons sunflower oil
1 medium red pepper	1 medium red bell pepper
2 tablespoons medium Madras curry powder	2 tablespoons medium Madras curry powder
2 tablespoons wholewheat flour	2 tablespoons wholewheat flour
1 eating apple	1 eating apple
1 banana	1 banana
15 fl oz (450ml) chicken or vegetable stock	2 cups chicken or vegetable stock
6 oz (175g) frozen mixed vegetables, e.g. carrots, sweetcorn, peas, beans	1½ cups frozen mixed vegetables, e.g. carrots, corn, peas, beans
1 lb (450g) cooked turkey meat, chopped	2 cups chopped cooked turkey meat
4 oz (100g) drained canned pineapple rings, chopped	½ cup drained canned pineapple rings, chopped
2 tablespoons plain yoghurt or fromage frais	2 tablespoons plain yoghurt or fromage frais

To serve
Freshly chopped parsley

1 Peel and chop the onion, then heat the oil in a large saucepan and sauté the onion for 5 minutes, until softened.

2 Meanwhile, deseed and roughly chop the red (bell) pepper, add it to the pan and continue to sauté for 2–3 minutes.

3 Stir in the curry powder with the flour. Cook, stirring, over a low heat for 1–2 minutes. Peel, core and chop the apple and peel and slice the banana. Add to the pan.

4 Gradually add the stock, stirring. Bring to the boil, stirring, then cover and simmer for 15 minutes.

5 Add the frozen vegetables with the turkey and pineapple. Simmer for 5 minutes then stir in the yoghurt or fromage frais.

6 Serve immediately, sprinkled with the chopped parsley.

Fresh Peaches with Strawberry Sauce

A light fruity dessert with a wonderful flavour and a low calorie count. Try serving this for a special dinner party or as a healthy treat for the family.

PREPARATION TIME: *15 mins*   FREEZING: *Not suitable*
COOKING TIME: —   SERVES: *4*
KCALS PER SERVING: *about 80*

Imperial (Metric)	American
4 large, ripe peaches	4 large, ripe peaches
12 oz (350g) strawberries, halved	2 cups strawberries, halved
2 teaspoons clear honey	2 teaspoons clear honey

To decorate
Fresh mint leaves

1 Put the peaches into a large bowl. Cover with boiling water and stand for 1–2 minutes. Drain and refresh under cold water, then remove peel.
2 Halve the peeled peaches and remove the stones. Arrange 2 peach halves on each of 4 side plates, rounded side uppermost.
3 Hull the strawberries and process to a purée in the food processor. Add the honey and process again, just to combine.
4 Divide the strawberry sauce between the 4 servings, pouring it evenly over the peaches. Decorate with mint leaves before serving.

MENU 4
Crisp-Topped Vegetable Gratin

This tasty potato and carrot gratin makes a delicious savoury meal. Serve with cold or hot Ratatouille (see page 73) or a mixed salad.

PREPARATION TIME: *20 mins*   FREEZING: *Not suitable*
COOKING TIME: *25 mins*   SERVES: *4*
KCALS PER SERVING: *about 257*

Imperial (Metric)	American
1½ lb (675g) potatoes	1½ pounds potatoes
2 medium carrots	2 medium carrots
1 tablespoon wholegrain mustard	1 tablespoon wholegrain mustard
5 tablespoons semi-skimmed milk	5 tablespoons low-fat milk
1 teaspoon dried oregano	1 teaspoon dried oregano
3 oz (75g) reduced-fat mature Cheddar cheese, grated	⅔ cup grated reduced-fat mature Cheddar cheese
3 spring onions	3 scallions
Freshly ground black pepper	Freshly ground black pepper
1 oz (25g) sunflower seeds	2 tablespoons sunflower seeds

1 Preheat the oven to gas mark 6, 400°F (200°C).
2 Peel and dice the potatoes and carrots and cook them together in boiling water, in one pan for 10–12 minutes, until tender. Drain and mash with a potato masher.
3 Beat the mustard, milk and oregano into the potato mixture with two thirds of the grated cheese.
4 Chop the spring onions (scallions) finely and fold in. Season lightly with the black pepper.
5 Turn into a fairly shallow dish and sprinkle with the remaining cheese and the sunflower seeds.
6 Bake near the top of the oven for about 15 minutes, until golden. Serve immediately.

Fruit Juice Set Dessert with Fresh Fruits

This moulded, set dessert makes a delicious finale to any meal, and has a fresh and summery flavour. Serve with low-fat fromage frais or the ice-cream on page 177.

PREPARATION TIME: *10 mins*   FREEZING: *Not suitable*
COOKING TIME: *7 mins*   SERVES: *4*
KCALS PER SERVING: *about 90*

Imperial (Metric)	American
1 pint (600ml) orange, apple and passion fruit juice, unsweetened	2½ cups orange, apple and passion fruit juice, unsweetened
1 teaspoon Gelozone, or any vegetable-based gelatin	1 teaspoon Kuzu, or any vegetable-based gelatin
2 tablespoons clear honey	2 tablespoons clear honey
Grated rind of 1 orange	Grated rind of 1 orange
2 kiwi fruit	2 kiwi fruit
1 ripe pear	1 ripe pear

1 Put the fruit juice into a saucepan and whisk in the gelatin.
2 Heat, stirring continuously until the mixture boils. Remove from the heat and set aside to cool for 10 minutes. Stir in the honey to dissolve, then stir in the orange rind.
3 Peel and slice the kiwi fruits and peel, core and slice the pear. Put into the base of a 1½ pint (900ml/3–3½ cup) mould.
4 Pass the mixture through a sieve over the fruit. Cool, then refrigerate until set.

MENU 5
Radicchio, Spinach and Chicken Salad with Walnuts

This is a simple yet filling salad which is low in fat. Serve with baked potatoes.

Radicchio is a cultivated variety of wild chicory (endive). Choose one with dark red leaves for this recipe.

PREPARATION TIME: *5 mins* FREEZING: *Not suitable*
COOKING TIME: — SERVES: *4*
KCALS PER SERVING: *about 223*

Imperial (Metric)	American
1 head radicchio	1 head radicchio
8 oz (225g) shredded young spinach leaves	5 cups shredded young spinach leaves
2 large oranges	2 large oranges
12 oz (350g) cooked, skinned chicken	1½ cups cooked, skinned chicken
2 oz (50g) diced walnuts	½ cup diced walnuts

For the dressing	**For the dressing**
2 tablespoons lime juice	2 tablespoons lime juice
2 teaspoons olive oil	2 teaspoons olive oil
1 clove garlic, crushed	1 clove garlic, crushed
1 tablespoon freshly chopped basil	1 tablespoon freshly chopped basil

1 Prepare the dressing: put the dressing ingredients into a small mixing bowl and whisk with a fork.
2 Roughly shred the radicchio leaves into a large salad bowl. Add the spinach.
3 Peel and segment the oranges and add them to the bowl with the chicken.
4 Pour the dressing over the salad and toss to coat. Serve immediately, sprinkled with the walnuts.

Mocha Fool

This is a luxurious quick dessert which is surprisingly low in calories.

PREPARATION TIME: *10 mins*   FREEZING: *Not suitable*
COOKING TIME: *5 mins*   SERVES: *4*
KCALS PER SERVING: *about 127*

Imperial (Metric)	*American*
10 fl oz (300ml) low-fat fromage frais	1¼ cups low-fat fromage frais
10 fl oz (300ml) Greek yoghurt	1¼ cups Greek yoghurt
2 tablespoons coffee liqueur	2 tablespoons coffee liqueur
2 oz (50g) plain carob, pieces	2 tablespoons chopped plain carob

1 Turn the fromage frais into a mixing bowl and stir in the yoghurt and liqueur.
2 Melt the carob in a bowl over a pan of simmering water or, if you have a microwave, microwave it in a bowl for 2–2½ minutes on a medium (40%) power, stirring every minute.
3 Stir the melted carob into the yoghurt mixture, then divide it between 4 sundae dishes. Chill until ready to serve.

MENU 6
Grilled Stuffed Trout with Savoury Rice

Trout is a filling fish with plenty of protein and vitamins A and D in the polyunsaturated fat it contains. The rice provides carbohydrate for energy and the B group of vitamins.

PREPARATION TIME: *15 mins*   FREEZING: *Not suitable*
COOKING TIME: *30 mins*   SERVES: *4*
KCALS PER SERVING: *about 390*

Imperial (Metric)	American
4 medium trout (6 oz (170g) each)	4 medium trout
Olive oil for brushing	Olive oil for brushing
14 oz (400g) can chopped tomatoes with herbs	14-ounce can chopped tomatoes with herbs

For the stuffing

1 small sweet eating apple	1 small sweet eating apple
3 oz (75g) fresh brown breadcrumbs	1½ cups fresh brown breadcrumbs
1 teaspoon lemon juice	1 teaspoon lemon juice
1 tablespoon freshly chopped parsley	1 tablespoon freshly chopped parsley
1 egg, beaten	1 egg, beaten

For the savoury rice

1 medium onion	1 medium onion
1 medium carrot	1 medium carrot
1 tablespoon sunflower oil	1 tablespoon sunflower oil
10 oz (275g) easy-cook brown rice	1½ cups easy-cook brown rice
1 pint (600ml) vegetable stock	2½ cups vegetable stock
1 small sweet eating apple	1 small sweet eating apple

1 Clean and gut the trout. To make the stuffing, core and chop the apple then put into a mixing bowl with the breadcrumbs, lemon juice and parsley. Mix with the beaten egg to bind. Divide the stuffing between the fish, pushing it well into each cavity.

2 Lightly oil the grill (broiler) rack and brush the fish lightly with corn oil. Grill (broil) under a low heat for about 7 minutes each side, or until cooked.

3 To prepare the savoury rice, peel and chop the onion then scrub and dice the carrot. Heat the oil in a medium pan, then sauté the onion and carrot for about 5 minutes, until the onion softens.

4 Add the rice and stir for 1 minute. Stir in the stock. Bring to the boil then cover and simmer for about 20 minutes, until the rice is tender and the liquid has been more or less absorbed. Peel, core and chop the apple and add to the rice.

5 Purée the can of tomatoes in a blender then heat slowly, stirring in a separate pan, until simmering.

6 Arrange the rice on a serving dish, top with the grilled trout and hand the tomato sauce round separately.

Oranges with Kirsch

High-fibre oranges are full of vitamin C and refreshing as a dessert. This recipe is so simple yet it tastes wonderful. Serve with plain yoghurt.

PREPARATION TIME: *15 mins*   FREEZING: *Not suitable*
COOKING TIME: *2 mins*   SERVES: *4*
KCALS PER SERVING: *about 117*

Imperial (Metric)	American
4 large oranges	4 large oranges
2 teaspoons drained and chopped Chinese stem ginger in syrup	2 teaspoons drained and chopped Chinese stem ginger in syrup
2 tablespoons kirsch	2 tablespoons kirsch

To serve
8 tablespoons set plain yoghurt

1 Remove the rind from 1 orange using a potato peeler, taking care not to remove any white pith.
2 Cut the rind into thin strips and place in a small pan. Cover with water, bring to the boil and simmer for 2 minutes. Set aside.
3 Remove the peel and pith from all the oranges, holding them over a bowl to catch any juice.
4 Slice the oranges thinly. Arrange in a shallow serving dish.
5 Pass peel through a sieve and add to the orange slices with the ginger. Pour over kirsch and any reserved orange juice.
6 Cover and refrigerate for 15 minutes for the flavours to develop, then serve with the yoghurt.

MENU 7
Special Chow Mein Stir Fry

Delicious Chinese chow mein can be low in calories providing you don't use too much oil. Like all stir-fry dishes ensure you have all the ingredients assembled and prepared before you start to cook.

PREPARATION TIME: *10 mins*   FREEZING: *Not suitable*
COOKING TIME: *12 mins*   SERVES: *4*
KCALS PER SERVING: *about 315*

Imperial (Metric)	*American*
1 bunch spring onions	1 bunch scallions
6 oz (175g) egg noodles	1¼ cups egg noodles
2 tablespoons olive oil	2 tablespoons olive oil
12 oz (350g) skinned and boned chicken breast, chopped	1½ cups chopped, skinned and boned chicken breast
8 oz (225g) fresh beansprouts	8 oz (225g) fresh beansprouts
4 oz (100g) peeled prawns	½ cup peeled shrimps
2 tablespoons light soy sauce	2 tablespoons light soy sauce
1 tablespoon sherry	1 tablespoon sherry
Juice of 1 orange	Juice of 1 orange

1 Chop the spring onions (scallions).
2 Place the noodles in a pan of boiling water. Simmer, stirring occasionally, for 3–4 mintues, then drain.
3 Meanwhile, heat the oil in a wok or large frying pan (skillet). Stir fry the spring onions (scallions) and chicken for 2–3 minutes. Stir in the drained noodles with the beansprouts, prawns (shrimps), soy sauce, sherry and orange juice.
4 Heat through thoroughly, stirring, then serve immediately.

Raspberry Fool

This high-fibre dessert may be made from fresh fruit when in season, but is also excellent made with frozen raspberries.

The dessert will keep in the fridge for up to 2 hours, but may also be served within 15 minutes of completing the preparation.

PREPARATION TIME: *10 mins*　FREEZING: *Not suitable*
COOKING TIME: —　SERVES: *4*
KCALS PER SERVING: *about 67*

Imperial (Metric)
12 oz (350g) raspberries
2 tablespoons raw cane
　sugar
5 oz (150g) carton low-fat
　plain yoghurt
3 tablespoons low-fat
　fromage frais

American
3 cups raspberries
2 tablespoons raw cane
　sugar
⅔ cup low-fat plain
　yoghurt
3 tablespoons low-fat
　fromage frais

To garnish
Fresh raspberries (optional)

1 Purée the raspberries in a blender then stir in the sugar to taste.
2 Fold in the yoghurt and fromage frais.
3 Transfer to 4 wine glasses and refrigerate until ready to serve.
4 Serve garnished with the fresh raspberries, if using.

MENU 8
Fish Provençal

Cod steaks are high in protein and low in fat. Cooked on a colourful mixture of Mediterranean vegetables they make a quick and filling dish. Serve with chunks of wholewheat bread to mop up the juices, and a mixed salad.

PREPARATION TIME: *15 mins* FREEZING: *Not suitable*
COOKING TIME: *45 mins* SERVES: *4*
KCALS PER SERVING: *about 224*

Imperial (Metric)
2 medium onions
1 red pepper
1 green pepper
2 tablespoons olive oil
2 cloves garlic, crushed
14 oz (400g) can chopped tomatoes
2 tablespoons tomato paste
1 teaspoon dried oregano or 1 tablespoon freshly chopped
A little sea salt and freshly ground black pepper
2 oz (50g) black olives, stoned
4 cod steaks (6 oz (175g) each)

American
2 medium onions
1 red bell pepper
1 green bell pepper
2 tablespoons olive oil
2 cloves garlic, crushed
14-ounce can chopped tomatoes
2 tablespoons tomato paste
1 teaspoon dried oregano or 1 tablespoon freshly chopped
A little sea salt and freshly ground black pepper
½ cup stoned black olives
4 medium cod steaks

1 Peel and slice the onions. Deseed and slice the (bell) peppers.
2 Heat the oil in a large frying pan (skillet) then sauté the onions for about 5 minutes, until softened.
3 Add the (bell) peppers and garlic and fry gently for 10 minutes, stirring frequently.
4 Add the tomatoes, tomato paste, oregano and a seasoning of salt and pepper.

5 Cover and simmer for 20 minutes then stir in the olives and arrange the cod steaks on the vegetables.
6 Cover the pan with a lid and continue to simmer for 5–7 minutes until the fish is cooked. Serve immediately.

Lemon Sorbet

Homemade water ice prepared with citrus fruits is tangy and refreshing. This lemon sorbet stores well in the freezer for up to 3 months and is very easy to prepare.

There is little food value in sorbet but the fresh orange segments provide fibre and vitamin C in this low-calorie dessert.

PREPARATION TIME: *15 mins*   FREEZING: *Suitable*
COOKING TIME: *10 mins*   SERVES: *4*
KCALS PER SERVING: *about 90*

Imperial (Metric)
3 large lemons
4 tablespoons clear honey
1 pint (600ml) water
2 egg whites

American
3 large lemons
4 tablespoons clear honey
2½ cups water
2 egg whites

To decorate:
2 oranges, segmented
  without pith, peel or
  membrane
Fresh sprigs of mint
  (optional)

1 Using a zester, remove the rind from 2 of the lemons and reserve, then squeeze the juice from all the lemons into a bowl. Set aside.
2 Put the honey and water into a large saucepan and bring to the boil, stirring until the honey dissolves. Simmer for 5 minutes then cool slightly.
3 Add the lemon zest and juice to the syrup. Stir well, then freeze in a fairly shallow container until mushy.
4 Turn into a large, cold bowl and beat with an electric beater until the mixture is almost white.
5 Beat the egg whites in a clean bowl until standing in soft peaks. Fold into the sorbet and freeze again until firm.
6 Before serving the sorbet, place it in the main part of the refrigerator for 30 minutes to improve the flavour.
7 Serve the sorbet in wine glasses, topped with the orange segments and decorated with the mint, if using.

ENTERTAINING ON IMPULSE

Unexpected guests, especially in large numbers, fill some people with trepidation as meal time approaches. The six menus in this chapter are for quick and easy three-course lunches or dinners that can be rustled up from healthy ingredients found in the fridge, store cupboard, freezer and vegetable rack.

Today's style of entertaining should be reasonably light on food and wine. People no longer enjoy waking up the following morning with that feeling of bloated over-indulgence which continues for most of the day, whilst their livers endeavour to cope with the onslaught of excess alcohol and rich, fatty foods consumed the previous evening.

It is perfectly acceptable to offer just two courses but I have included starters as these particular ones are very easy to put together, and by serving a starter you do instantly transform a meal into an occasion. If you prefer, you could serve two or three starters together with a selection of fresh fruits and bread and present the meal buffet style. Whichever way you choose, I sincerely hope that this section takes the worry out of entertaining so you can relax and enjoy your friends' company, as after all, that is what socializing is all about.

MENU 1
Orange and Walnut Salad

This attractive salad with its creamy but low-fat dressing makes a delicious healthy starter which is quick and easy to prepare. Oranges add fibre, colour and vitamin C whilst the nuts add protein.

PREPARATION TIME: *15 mins*   FREEZING: *Not suitable*
COOKING TIME: —   SERVES: *4*

Imperial (Metric)	*American*
½ iceberg lettuce	½ iceberg lettuce
3 oz (75g) watercress	3 cups watercress
2 oranges	2 oranges
6 fl oz (175ml) low-fat fromage frais	¾ cup low-fat fromage frais
Freshly ground black pepper	Freshly ground black pepper
1 teaspoon wholegrain mustard	1 teaspoon granary mustard
2 teaspoons freshly chopped chives	2 teaspoons freshly chopped chives
2 oz (50g) walnuts, chopped	½ cup chopped walnuts

1 Cut the lettuce into 4 wedges and arrange on 4 plates.
2 Divide the watercress between the plates, then peel and segment the oranges, discarding the pith and holding the fruit over a bowl as you prepare them, so that you catch any juice. Add the orange segments to the salad.
3 Mix together the juice from the oranges with the fromage frais, black pepper to taste and the mustard. Spoon over the salad.
4 Sprinkle with the chives and walnuts and serve immediately.

Golden Pasta Bake

Serve this tasty pasta dish for lunch or supper. Accompany with a mixed salad or coleslaw made with a low-fat dressing for a complete meal.

PREPARATION TIME: *15 mins* FREEZING: *Suitable*
COOKING TIME: *50 mins* SERVES: *4*

Imperial (Metric)
1 large onion
2 sticks celery
2 tablespoons sunflower oil
1 clove garlic, crushed
8 oz (225g) button mushrooms, sliced
8 oz (225g) broccoli spears, roughly chopped
14 oz (400g) can chopped tomatoes with herbs
2 tablespoons tomato paste
Freshly ground black pepper
12 oz (350g) wholewheat pasta twists
3 tablespoons wholewheat flour
1 pint (600ml) semi-skimmed milk
1 oz (25g) butter
2 eggs
6 oz (175g) Emmenthal cheese, grated

American
1 large onion
2 sticks celery
2 tablespoons sunflower oil
1 clove garlic, crushed
2 cups sliced button mushrooms
2 cups roughly chopped broccoli spears
14-ounce can chopped tomatoes with herbs
2 tablespoons tomato paste
Freshly ground black pepper
4½ cups wholewheat pasta twists
3 tablespoons wholewheat flour
2½ cups low-fat milk
2 tablespoons butter
2 eggs
1½ cups grated Swiss cheese

1 Preheat the oven to gas mark 6, 200°C (400°F).
2 Peel and chop the onion and chop the celery.
3 Heat the oil in a medium-sized saucepan, then sauté the garlic with the onion and celery for about 5 minutes, or until softened.

4 Stir in the mushrooms and continue to sauté for a further 5 minutes.

5 Add the broccoli with the chopped tomatoes and the tomato paste. Season with a little black pepper then gradually stir in 5 fl oz (150ml/⅔ cup) cold water. Bring to the boil, then simmer covered, for 15 minutes.

6 Meanwhile, cook the pasta in plenty of boiling water for about 10-12 minutes, until *al dente*.

7 Make the sauce: blend the flour with a little of the milk in a medium-sized nonstick pan. Add the remaining milk with the butter.

8 Heat gently, whisking continuously until the sauce boils and thickens.

9 Beat the eggs together with a fork, then stir into the sauce.

10 Turn the vegetable mixture into a gratin dish. Top with the freshly cooked, drained pasta.

11 Pour over the sauce to coat evenly, then sprinkle over the grated cheese.

12 Bake for 20 minutes, until the topping is golden.

Poppyseed Pudding with Apricot Sauce

This light and fruity pudding contains plenty of fibre. It cooks superfast in the microwave or can be baked in a conventional oven if preferred.

PREPARATION TIME: *10 mins*   FREEZING: *Suitable at end of stage 6*
COOKING TIME: *7 mins or 40 mins*   SERVES: *4*

Imperial (Metric)	*American*
4 oz (100g) self-raising wholewheat flour	1 cup self-rising wholewheat flour
1 teaspoon baking powder	1 teaspoon baking powder
3 fl oz (85ml) sunflower oil	1/3 cup sunflower oil
2 oz (50g) raw cane sugar	4 tablespoons raw cane sugar
2 eggs, beaten	2 eggs, beaten
Grated rind of 1 lemon	Grated rind of 1 lemon
1 tablespoon poppy seeds	1 tablespoon poppy seeds
3 tablespoons semi-skimmed milk	3 tablespoons low-fat milk

For the apricot sauce

1 teaspoon arrowroot	1 teaspoon arrowroot
Juice of 1 large orange	Juice of 1 large orange
3 tablespoons reduced sugar apricot jam	3 tablespoons reduced sugar apricot jam

To decorate
3 thin orange slices, quartered

1 If using the oven preheat it to gas mark 4, 350°F (180°C). Base line and grease a 2 pint (1.1 litre/5 cup) pudding basin.
2 Sift the flour and baking powder into a large mixing bowl. Add all the remaining ingredients for the pudding.
3 Beat together, using a wooden spoon, for 2 minutes then pour into the prepared pudding basin.

4 If cooking in a conventional oven bake for approximately 40 minutes, until a skewer inserted in the centre comes out clean.

5 If using a microwave, cover the basin with cling film and microwave on 100% (full power) for 5–7 minutes, or until a wooden cocktail stick inserted in the centre comes out clean.

6 Leave to stand for 5 minutes while making the sauce.

7 Blend the arrowroot to a smooth paste with 1 tablespoon cold water. Put the orange juice and jam into a jug if using a microwave or into a small pan if using a conventional oven. Add the blended arrowroot.

8 Microwave on 100% (full power) for 2 minutes, stirring well after 1 minute and at the end of the cooking time. If using a conventional oven, bring the pan to simmering point, stirring continuously. Simmer for 1–2 minutes.

9 Turn the pudding out on to a serving dish, decorate with the quartered orange slices and serve with the sauce.

MENU 2
Avocado Dip

Dark purple or rich green avocado pears are the fruit of
the avocado tree, and when ripe they have soft, creamy
flesh which is rich in oil, vitamins A, B, C, D, E and
potassium. As the avocado is fairly high in
monounsaturated fats it's best to mix it with low-fat
ingredients such as the cottage cheese used in this dip.

PREPARATION TIME: *10 mins*   FREEZING: *Not suitable*
COOKING TIME: —   SERVES: *4*

Imperial (Metric)	American
1 large ripe avocado pear	1 large ripe avocado pear
5 oz cottage cheese	⅔ cup cottage cheese
1 teaspoon lemon juice	1 teaspoon lemon juice
1 tablespoon freshly chopped parsley	1 tablespoon freshly chopped parsley
Freshly ground black pepper	Freshly ground black pepper

To serve
 Sticks of raw vegetables
  such as carrots, celery,
  baby corn

1 Peel and dice the avocado, discarding the stone.
2 Put the avocado into a food processor and process until
  puréed.
3 Add the cottage cheese, lemon juice and parsley. Blend
  until smooth.
4 Season to taste with black pepper.
5 Transfer to a serving dish and serve immediately with
  the vegetable sticks.

Stuffed Mushrooms

Large flat mushrooms with a savoury filling are extremely popular and surprisingly sustaining. Serve 2 per person for a main course with a bowl of tossed mixed salad and warm wholemeal rolls.

PREPARATION TIME: *15 mins*   FREEZING: *Not suitable*
COOKING TIME: *15 mins*   SERVES: *4*

Imperial (Metric)	American
8 large flat mushrooms	8 large flat mushrooms
4 tablespoons olive oil	4 tablespoons olive oil
4 spring onions	4 scallions
8 tablespoons wholewheat breadcrumbs	8 tablespoons wholewheat breadcrumbs
1 tablespoon freshly chopped parsley	1 tablespoon freshly chopped parsley
4 oz (100g) frozen sweetcorn	1 cup frozen corn
1 tablespoon Worcestershire sauce	1 tablespoon Worcestershire sauce
3 oz (75g) reduced-fat mature Cheddar cheese, grated	⅔ cup grated reduced-fat mature Cheddar cheese

1 Preheat the oven to gas mark 6, 400°F (200°C).
2 Gently pull the stalks from the mushrooms then brush the mushroom caps on both sides with a little of the oil and stand them on 2 baking sheets, gill side up.
3 Chop the stalks, then heat the remaining oil in a large frying pan (skillet). Roughly chop the spring onions (scallions) and fry for 2 minutes. Add the mushroom stalks, breadcrumbs, parsley, corn and Worcestershire sauce and mix well.
4 Divide the filling between the prepared mushroom caps. Sprinkle with the grated cheese then bake for 12 minutes, until golden.

Plums with Port

Plums provide fibre and are delicious hot or cold. The port makes this dessert really special but it can be left out if you prefer. Serve with low-fat fromage frais or yoghurt and sprinkle with a little granola (see page 150) if you wish.

PREPARATION TIME: *15 mins*   FREEZING: *Not suitable*
COOKING TIME: *5–10 mins*   SERVES: *4*

Imperial (Metric)	American
1 lb (450g) dessert plums	1 pound dessert plums
5 fl oz (150ml) apple juice	⅔ cup apple juice
1 tablespoon clear honey	1 tablespoon clear honey
2 tablespoons port	2 tablespoons port

1 Halve and stone the plums and put them into a saucepan with the apple juice and honey.
2 Bring very slowly, just to the boil, then cover and simmer for about 5–10 minutes, until fairly soft.
3 Turn into a serving dish. Add the port, then serve warm or cold with fromage frais or yoghurt.

MENU 3
Light Mushroom Soup

Try this light version of mushroom soup made without heavy cream and egg yolks. It's the ideal way to start a meal.

PREPARATION TIME: *15 mins*   FREEZING: *Suitable at end of stage 3*
COOKING TIME: *25 mins*   SERVES: *4*

Imperial (Metric)	American
1 small onion	1 small onion
8 oz (225g) button mushrooms, sliced	4 cups sliced button mushrooms
1 pint (600ml) vegetable stock	2½ cups vegetable stock
5 fl oz (150ml) semi-skimmed milk	⅔ cup low-fat milk
2 tablespoons fromage frais	2 tablespoons fromage frais
2 tablespoons sherry (optional)	2 tablespoons sherry (optional)

To garnish
Freshly chopped chives

1 Peel and chop the onion then put it into a large pan with the mushrooms and half the stock. Bring to the boil, then cover and simmer for 20 minutes. Allow to cool slightly.
2 Blend the contents of the pan until the onion and mushrooms are very finely chopped. Return to the pan.
3 Gradually stir in the remaining stock with the milk. Slowly bring to simmering point, stirring continuously. Remove the pan from the heat.
4 Stir in the fromage frais and sherry, if using. Serve immediately, garnished with the chopped chives.

Easy Wholewheat Pizza

A pizza made quickly from energy-giving wholewheat
flour and a little polyunsaturated margarine is both filling
and nutritious. Serve this appetizing supper dish with the
Curried Kidney Bean and Sweetcorn Salad on page 77 or
the Sunny Vegetables Mediterranean Style on page 74.

PREPARATION TIME: *20 mins*   FREEZING: *Suitable*
COOKING TIME: *25 mins*   SERVES: *4*

Imperial (Metric)

For the topping
1 medium onion
2 tablespoons olive oil
1 clove garlic, crushed
4 oz (100g) button
   mushrooms, sliced
1 teaspoon dried mixed
   herbs or 1 tablespoon
   freshly chopped
A little sea salt and freshly
   ground black pepper
14 oz (400g) can chopped
   tomatoes
2 tablespoons tomato paste
6 oz (175g) reduced-fat
   Cheddar cheese, grated
2 oz (50g) pimento-stuffed
   olives, sliced

For the base
8 oz (225g) self-raising
   wholewheat flour
2 oz (50g) polyunsaturated
   margarine
5 fl oz (150ml) semi-
   skimmed milk

American

For the topping
1 medium onion
2 tablespoons olive oil
1 clove garlic, crushed
1 cup sliced button
   mushrooms
1 teaspoon dried mixed
   herbs or 1 tablespoon
   freshly chopped
A little sea salt and freshly
   ground black pepper
14-ounce can chopped
   tomatoes
2 tablespoons tomato paste
1½ cups grated reduced-fat
   Cheddar cheese
½ cup sliced pimento-stuffed
   olives

For the base
2 cups self-rising
   wholewheat flour
4 tablespoons
   polyunsaturated margarine
⅔ cup low-fat
   milk

1 Preheat the oven to gas mark 7, 425°F (220°C).
2 Peel and chop the onion.
3 Heat 1 tablespoon of the oil in a frying pan (skillet), then fry the garlic with the onion and mushrooms for about 5 minutes, until the onion softens.
4 Stir in the herbs with a little seasoning, the chopped tomatoes and the tomato paste. Simmer uncovered, stirring occasionally, for 15 minutes, until a fairly thick sauce results.
5 Meanwhile, prepare the base. Put the flour into a mixing bowl. Rub in the margarine until the mixture resembles fine breadcrumbs.
6 Add the milk and mix to form a soft dough. Knead lightly then roll out to 20cm (8in) circle. Arrange on a lightly greased baking sheet.
7 Spread the tomato mixture evenly over the pizza base. Sprinkle with the grated cheese then top with the sliced olives. Pour the remaining tablespoon of olive oil all over the pizza.
8 Bake in the preheated oven for 10 minutes, then reduce the heat to gas mark 6, 400°F (200°C) and bake for a further 10–15 minutes, until golden.

Raspberry and Blackcurrant Compote with Yoghurt

Summer fruits stewed briefly with a little honey taste wonderful, provide vitamin C and fibre, and look fantastic served with the white Greek yoghurt. Remember that creamy Greek yoghurt does contain 10% animal fat, so be careful not to overindulge in the topping.

PREPARATION TIME: *10 mins*   FREEZING: *Not suitable*
COOKING TIME: *15 mins*   SERVES: *4*

Imperial (Metric)	*American*
1 lb (450g) mixed raspberries and blackcurrants, fresh or frozen	1 pound fresh or frozen mixed raspberries and blackcurrants
3 tablespoons clear honey	3 tablespoons clear honey

For the yoghurt

3 tablespoons pure, unsweetened orange juice	3 tablespoons pure, unsweetened orange juice
8 fl oz (250ml) Greek yoghurt	1 cup Greek yoghurt
1 egg white	1 egg white

1 Put the raspberries, blackcurrants and honey into a heavy-based pan with 4 fl oz (120ml/½ cup) water. Cook gently for 10–15 minutes, stirring occasionally, until the fruit is tender.
2 Turn into a serving dish and set aside to cool.
3 Mix the orange juice with the yoghurt.
4 Whisk the egg white until stiff, then fold it into the yoghurt mixture. Serve immediately with the cooled compote.

MENU 4
Avocado Salads

The flavours of avocado and melon complement each other well. Coating the avocado with the dressing immediately it has been diced helps prevent it going brown, so you can prepare the starter about 30 minutes before you are due to serve the meal.

PREPARATION TIME: *20 mins* FREEZING: *Not suitable*
COOKING TIME: — SERVES: *4*

Imperial (Metric)	American
1 large avocado	1 large avocado
½ cantaloupe melon	½ cantaloupe melon

For the dressing

2 tablespoons lime juice	2 tablespoons lime juice
3 tablespoons sunflower oil	3 tablespoons sunflower oil
2 teaspoons cider vinegar	2 teaspoons cider vinegar
2 teaspoons freshly chopped mint	2 teaspoons freshly chopped mint
Freshly ground black pepper	Freshly ground black pepper

To serve
Little Gem lettuce leaves
Sprigs of watercress

1 Put all the ingredients for the dressing into a bowl and whisk with a fork.
2 Peel, stone and dice the avocado and toss in the dressing.
3 Either ball the melon, using a melon baller, or peel and dice the flesh.
4 Arrange lettuce leaves and watercress sprigs on 4 side plates or in bowls.
5 Top with the melon then the avocado. Pour over any remaining dressing and serve.

Mediterranean Lentil Stew

Lentils are a valuable source of protein and have been a
staple food in Middle Eastern countries, particularly
Egypt, for centuries. Lentils contain carbohydrate,
thiamin, iron and calcium.

Serve with wholewheat bread and salad.

PREPARATION TIME: *20 mins*　FREEZING: *Suitable*
COOKING TIME: *45 mins*　SERVES: *4*

Imperial (Metric)	American
1 medium onion	1 medium onion
2 celery stalks	2 celery stalks
1 green pepper	1 green bell pepper
1 red pepper	1 red bell pepper
2 tablespoons olive oil	2 tablespoons olive oil
2 cloves garlic, crushed	2 cloves garlic, crushed
8 oz (225g) red lentils, washed	1½ cups red lentils, washed
2 tablespoons tomato paste	2 tablespoons tomato paste
1½ pints (750ml) vegetable stock	3 cups vegetable stock
1 teaspoon dried oregano or 1 tablespoon freshly chopped	1 teaspoon dried oregano or 1 tablespoon freshly chopped
2 oz (50g) raisins	½ cup raisins
2 tablespoons freshly chopped parsley	2 tablespoons freshly chopped parsley
4 oz (100g) frozen peas	1 cup frozen peas

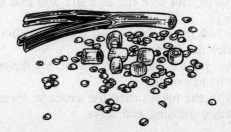

1 Peel and chop the onion, chop the celery stalks, and deseed and chop the green and red (bell) peppers.
2 Heat the oil in a large saucepan. Add the onion, celery, (bell) peppers and garlic. Sauté for about 7 minutes, until the vegetables soften and start to brown round the edges a little.
3 Add the lentils and stir to coat with the oil.
4 Blend the tomato paste with a little of the stock, then add it to the pan with the remaining stock, the oregano and the raisins.
5 Bring to the boil, then cover and simmer for 35 minutes until the lentils are tender and mushy. Stir the parsley and peas into the pan 5 minutes before the end of the cooking time. Serve immediately.

Fruity Granola

Granola is a sort of toasted muesli, which stores well in an airtight container and is a wonderful standby when guests arrive unexpectedly. Serve with all sorts of fruit or yoghurt, or simply pour ice-cold milk over it.

This version of granola is high in fibre and low on added sugar.

PREPARATION TIME: *15 mins*   FREEZING: *Not suitable*
COOKING TIME: *35 mins*   SERVES: *4–6*

Imperial (Metric)	American
3 fl oz (85ml) sunflower oil	⅓ cup sunflower oil
3 tablespoons malt extract	3 tablespoons malt extract
4 tablespoons clear honey	4 tablespoons clear honey
4 oz (100g) blanched almonds	¾ cup blanched almonds
1 lb (450g) rolled oats	4 cups rolled oats
2 oz (50g) sunflower seeds	3 tablespoons sunflower seeds
4 oz (100g) 1 cup chopped dried apricots	1 cup chopped dried apricots
2 oz (50g) raisins	½ cup raisins
2 oz (50g) chopped dates	½ cup chopped dates

1 Preheat the oven to gas mark 5, 375°F (190°C).
2 Put the oil, malt extract and honey into a large pan and heat gently, stirring until liquid.
3 Roughly chop the almonds.
4 Mix the almonds, oats and sunflower seeds into the oil mixture. Turn into a large roasting pan and bake for approximately 30 minutes, stirring twice during this time.
5 Set aside until completely cold, then break the pieces up with your fingers. Stir in the apricots, raisins and dates. Store in an airtight container.

MENU 5
Tomato and Herb Gratin

This warming low-fat starter is particularly quick and easy to make yet tastes as though you spent hours preparing it.

Tomatoes provide vitamin C and a little fibre, and the cheese adds protein. Serve with warmed wholewheat rolls.

PREPARATION TIME: *20 mins*   FREEZING: *Not suitable*
COOKING TIME: *10 mins*   SERVES: *4*

Imperial (Metric)	American
1 lb (450g) ripe tomatoes	1 pound ripe tomatoes
2 medium onions	2 medium onions
2 cloves garlic	2 cloves garlic
1 tablespoon olive oil	1 tablespoon olive oil
1 tablespoon freshly chopped oregano	1 tablespoon freshly chopped oregano
Few chives, chopped	Few chives, chopped
A little sea salt and freshly ground black pepper	A little sea salt and freshly ground black pepper
2 oz (50g) reduced-fat Cheddar cheese, grated	½ cup grated reduced-fat Cheddar cheese
1 oz (25g) wholewheat breadcrumbs	½ cup wholewheat breadcrumbs

1 Peel the tomatoes, then chop them roughly, discarding the seeds and hard core.
2 Peel and chop the onions and garlic.
3 Heat the oil in a medium saucepan, add the onions and garlic and sauté for about 5 minutes, until softened.
4 Add the tomatoes and stir over a medium heat until warmed through. Stir the oregano and chives into the tomatoes and season lightly with the sea salt and pepper.

5 Divide the tomato mixture between 4 ramekin dishes.
6 Combine the cheese and breadcrumbs and sprinkle evenly over the tomato mixture.
7 Brown under a preheated medium grill (broiler) and serve immediately with wholewheat rolls.

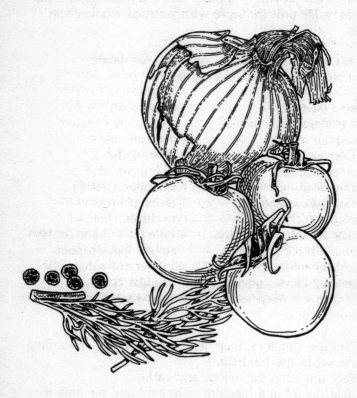

Garlicky Aubergine Pâté

Aubergines (eggplants) are a good source of dietary fibre, and are low in calories as long as they are not cooked with a vast amount of oil, as is often the case. Serve with Royal Salad (page 76) and warm pitta bread.

PREPARATION TIME: *20 mins*   FREEZING: *Not suitable*
COOKING TIME: *35 mins*   SERVES: *4*

Imperial (Metric)	American
2 medium aubergines	2 medium eggplants
2 cloves garlic, crushed	2 cloves garlic, crushed
1 tablespoon olive oil	1 tablespoon olive oil
2 tablespoons semi-skimmed milk	2 tablespoons low-fat milk
1 teaspoon curry powder	1 teaspoon curry powder
A little sea salt	A little sea salt

1 Preheat the oven to gas mark 4, 350°F (180°C).
2 Prick the aubergines (eggplants) two or three times each with a fork and stand on a baking sheet.
3 Bake for 30–35 minutes, or until tender. Allow to cool for 5–10 minutes, peel, and roughly chop flesh.
4 Put the flesh into a blender with the garlic, oil, milk, curry powder and salt. Blend to a purée.
5 Turn into a shallow dish and leave to cool. Serve with salad and pitta bread.

Fresh and Dried Fruits Platter

A selection of fresh fruits in season, mixed with a few
dried fruits, such as dates, figs, apricots or raisins, looks
wonderful arranged on a large oval dish. Place it in the
centre of the table and allow guests to help themselves,
giving each person a side plate and knife plus a finger
bowl. Offer a large bowl of fromage frais or plain yoghurt
separately.

MENU 6
Sautéed Garlic Mushrooms

This tasty starter is simplicity itself to prepare and cook. I guarantee it will be extremely popular with nearly everyone.

PREPARATION TIME: *10 mins*   FREEZING: *Not suitable*
COOKING TIME: *10 mins*   SERVES: *4*

Imperial (Metric)	American
1 lb (450g) button mushrooms	1 pound button mushrooms
1 bunch spring onions	1 bunch scallions
1 oz (25g) butter	2 tablespoons butter
3 tablespoons olive oil	3 tablespoons olive oil
2 cloves garlic, crushed	2 cloves garlic, crushed

To garnish
Freshly chopped parsley

1 Trim the mushrooms and halve them if they are a little on the large side. Roughly chop the spring onions (scallions).
2 Heat the butter and oil in a large frying pan (skillet). Add the garlic, spring onions (scallions) and mushrooms and sauté over a medium heat until the mushrooms start to brown.
3 Serve immediately in warm ramekin dishes, garnished with the chopped parsley and accompanied with chunks of wholewheat bread.

Curried Chicken Toasted Sandwiches

Toasted sandwiches are always popular, and they're quick and easy to prepare too. Try this curried chicken version next time guests arrive unexpectedly – they're low in fat and high in protein and vitamin B. As an even quicker alternative serve as open sandwiches garnished with salad leaves.

PREPARATION TIME: *15 mins*   FREEZING: *Not suitable*
COOKING TIME: *5 mins*   SERVES: *4*

Imperial (Metric)	*American*
8 oz (225g) cold cooked chicken breast without skin	1 cup cold cooked chicken breast without skin
2 tablespoons reduced-fat mayonnaise	2 tablespoons reduced-fat mayonnaise
2 tablespoons low-fat plain yoghurt	2 tablespoons low-fat plain yoghurt
1 teaspoon mango chutney	1 teaspoon mango chutney
½ teaspoon curry powder	½ teaspoon curry powder
8 large slices wholewheat bread	8 large slices wholewheat bread
Low-fat spread (optional)	Low-fat spread (optional)

To serve
Salad garnish

1 Roughly chop the chicken and put it into a mixing bowl.
2 In a separate small bowl combine the mayonnaise with the yoghurt, chutney and curry powder. Mix well.
3 Pour the mayonnaise mixture over the chicken and stir to combine.
4 Spread the bread with the low-fat spread, if using, then divide the filling between 4 slices of bread and top with the remaining 4 slices to form 4 sandwiches.
5 Toast both sides of the sandwiches under a preheated medium grill (broiler), until golden.
6 Serve immediately with the salad garnish.

Nectarines and Grapefruit with Cointreau

This fresh, fruity dessert is very quick to prepare and can be served with plain yoghurt or fromage frais. If you don't want to use alcohol any fruit juice will do, such as grape, mandarin, apricot, orange or apple.

PREPARATION TIME: *20 mins*   FREEZING: *Not suitable*
COOKING TIME: —   SERVES: *4*

Imperial (Metric)	American
2 pink grapefruit	2 pink grapefruit
3 large nectarines	3 large nectarines
2 tablespoons Cointreau	2 tablespoons Cointreau

To serve
Yoghurt or fromage frais

1 Using a potato peeler, remove the rind from one grapefruit, being careful not to remove any white pith. Cut this rind into very thin strips and simmer in a little boiling water for 1–2 minutes, until softened. Drain and set aside.

2 Peel both grapefruit, holding them over a bowl to catch any drips. Segment the grapefruit, discarding the inner membrane, and put into the bowl. Squeeze out the membranes into the bowl before you discard them.

3 Segment the nectarines and add to the bowl. Pour over the Cointreau. Cover and refrigerate for at least 15 minutes for the flavours to mingle.

4 Serve the fruit, with the juices poured over, in individual serving dishes, topped with the yoghurt or fromage frais. Decorate with the strips of blanched peel.

PANIC-FREE PUDDINGS

A meal often doesn't feel complete without some sort of a dessert to round the whole thing off, but these days we demand light ones that can be put together fast. Many of the desserts in this chapter are based on fresh fruit and they almost all use everyday ingredients, presented in slightly unusual ways, so you should find an easy sweet for every occasion.

Avocado and Green Fruit Salad

Melon, avocado and green grapes make a wonderful and unusual combination. The fruit syrup is made from honey and lime juice for a delicious flavour.

PREPARATION TIME: *20 mins*   FREEZING: *Not suitable*
COOKING TIME: *20 mins chill time*   SERVES: *4–6*

Imperial (Metric)	American
1 Galia melon	1 Galia melon
8 oz (225g) seedless green grapes	1⅓ cups seedless green grapes
1 ripe avocado	1 ripe avocado

For the syrup

Imperial (Metric)	American
5 fl oz (150ml) water	⅔ cup water
2 tablespoons clear honey	2 tablespoons clear honey
Juice of 1 lime, strained	Juice of 1 lime, strained

1 Prepare the syrup first: put the water and honey into a small pan and heat, stirring, until the honey dissolves. Bring to the boil then remove the pan from the heat and leave to cool completely. Add the lime juice and pour into a serving bowl.
2 Halve and deseed the melon then cut into wedges and peel. Dice the flesh and add to the syrup with the grapes. Allow to stand for 20 minutes for the flavours to mingle.
3 Just before serving, halve and stone the avocado. Cut into quarters then peel and chop the flesh. Add to the fruit salad and serve immediately.

Summer Fruits in Grape Juice

Summer fruits marinated in grape juice for 40 minutes or
so before serving make a delicious high-fibre sweet with
very little work. Three varieties are quite adequate for an
impressive dessert. Serve with low-fat fromage frais or
plain yoghurt.

PREPARATION TIME: *15 mins*   FREEZING: *Not suitable*
COOKING TIME: *40 mins chill time*   SERVES: *4–6*

Imperial (Metric)	American
3 nectarines	3 nectarines
8 oz (225g) strawberries	2 cups strawberries
8 oz (225g) redcurrants	1⅓ cups redcurrants
10 fl oz (300ml) red grape juice	1¼ cups red grape juice
1 tablespoon clear honey	1 tablespoon clear honey

1 Halve the nectarines, and twist to remove the stone.
  Chop the nectarines roughly and put into a serving
  bowl. Halve the strawberries and add to the bowl.
  Remove the redcurrants from their stems and add to
  the bowl.
2 Stir the grape juice gradually into the honey, then pour
  over the fruits. Cover the bowl and refrigerate for
  40 minutes before serving.

Greek Yoghurt Surprise

Dried apricots and raisins soaked overnight in a little cider are deliciously moist and sweet. For this simple dessert they are topped with rich and creamy Greek yoghurt.

PREPARATION TIME: *15 mins + chill time*   FREEZING: *Not suitable*
COOKING TIME: —   SERVES: *4*

Imperial (Metric)	*American*
4 dried apricots	4 dried apricots
2 oz (50g) raisins	½ cup raisins
8 tablespoons medium-dry cider	8 tablespoons medium-dry cider
8 fl oz (250ml) Greek yoghurt	1 cup Greek yoghurt
2 oz (50g) toasted almonds	½ cup toasted almonds
2 teaspoons raw cane sugar	2 teaspoons raw cane sugar

1 Chop the apricots roughly and divide evenly between 4 ramekins or similar dishes. Add the raisins.
2 Pour 2 tablespoons cider over each dish of dried fruit. Cover and refrigerate for 24 hours.
3 Just before serving, top the fruits with the yoghurt and sprinkle with the toasted almonds and sugar.

Celebration Mango Foam

A light, mousse-like dessert that tastes creamy, with a hint of spice. Ideal for a dinner party.

PREPARATION TIME: *20 mins*   FREEZING: *Not suitable*
COOKING TIME: *20 mins chill time*   SERVES: *4*

Imperial (Metric)	*American*
1 orange	1 orange
2 medium-sized ripe mangos	2 medium-sized ripe mangos
2 egg whites	2 egg whites

To decorate
4 strawberries

1 Using a zester, remove the zest from half the orange and set aside. Squeeze the juice from the orange and put it into a food processor.
2 Peel the mangoes over a plate to catch any juice, then slice the flesh from the central stone in large pieces. Add the mango, with its juices, to the blender and purée until smooth. Pour into a bowl.
3 Whisk the egg whites until standing in soft peaks then fold them into the mango mixture, using a metal spoon.
4 Spoon the foam into 4 wine glasses and refrigerate for 20 minutes.
5 Serve decorated with the orange zest and the strawberries, cut into fans.

Apricot and Banana Splash

Dried apricots are high in fibre and a reasonable source of vitamin A, iron, and potassium. Serve this filling dessert with low-fat yoghurt or fromage frais.

PREPARATION TIME: *10 mins* FREEZING: *Not suitable*
COOKING TIME: *12 or 25 mins* SERVES: *4*

Imperial (Metric)	American
9 oz (250g) ready-soaked dried apricots	2¼ cups ready-soaked dried apricots
15 fl oz (450ml) water	2 cups water
5 fl oz (150ml) medium-sweet white wine	⅔ cup medium-sweet white wine
1 slice fresh lemon	1 slice fresh lemon
2 tablespoons clear honey	2 tablespoons clear honey
1 banana	1 banana

1 Wash the apricots and put them into a medium-sized saucepan, or if you have a microwave put them into a suitable bowl.
2 Add the water (in the case of microwave cooking, use boiling water), wine, lemon and honey and stir well.
3 Bring to the boil, then simmer, covered, for 25 minutes, until tender. If using a microwave, cover the bowl and microwave on 100% (full power) for 12 minutes, stirring once after 6 minutes.
4 Transfer to a serving dish and allow to cool completely. Remove the lemon.
5 Just before serving stir in the sliced banana.

Apple Sponge

A filling dessert made with wholewheat flour and apples for fibre and a reduced amount of fat and sugar. Serve piping hot with the Orange Sauce on page 165.

PREPARATION TIME: *15 mins*   FREEZING: *Suitable without the orange sauce*
COOKING TIME: *40 mins*   SERVES: *4–6*

You will need a 1½ pint (900ml/3¾ cup) soufflé dish, well greased.

Imperial (Metric)	American
1 medium-sized cooking apple	1 medium-sized cooking apple
3 oz (75g) polyunsaturated margarine, at room temperature	6 tablespoons polyunsaturated margarine, at room temperature
3 oz (75g) raw cane sugar	½ cup raw cane sugar
4 oz (100g) self-raising wholewheat flour	1 cup self-rising wholewheat flour
Grated rind of ½ orange	Grated rind of ½ orange
2 eggs, beaten	2 eggs, beaten
1 tablespoon orange juice	1 tablespoon orange juice

1 Preheat the oven to gas mark 4, 350°F (180°C).
2 Peel, core and roughly chop the apple.
3 Put the margarine, sugar, flour, orange rind and eggs into a large mixing bowl then beat together with an electric whisk, if available; if not a wooden spoon will do. Beat for about 1½ minutes until you have a creamy mixture.
4 Beat in the orange juice, then fold in the apple.
5 Turn the mixture into the soufflé dish and level off the surface.
6 Bake in the centre of the oven for about 40 minutes, until a skewer inserted in the centre comes out clean and the pudding is starting to shrink from the sides of the dish. Serve with Orange Sauce.

Orange Sauce

This sauce is made from fresh orange juice, lemon rind and honey, so it has a reasonable vitamin C content and is not too sweet. Serve hot over puddings and reduced fat and sugar ice-cream.

PREPARATION TIME: *10 mins*   FREEZING: *Not suitable*
COOKING TIME: *5 mins*   SERVES: *4*

Imperial (Metric)	American
2 teaspoons arrowroot	2 teaspoons arrowroot
Juice of 2 large oranges	Juice of 2 large oranges
Grated rind of 1 large lemon	Grated rind of 1 large lemon
1 tablespoon clear honey	1 tablespoon clear honey

1 Blend the arrowroot with the orange juice in a measuring jug, then make the liquid up to 7 fl oz (200ml/¾ cup) with water if necessary.
2 Pour into a medium-sized saucepan and add the lemon rind and honey. Bring to the boil, stirring.
3 Simmer for 1–2 minutes, stirring, then serve.

Poached Spiced Apples

Apples poached in grape juice with raisins and spices are filling but low in calories. Serve warm or cold with custard made from semi-skimmed (low-fat) milk and half the usual amount of sugar, or with plain yoghurt.

PREPARATION TIME: *15 mins*   FREEZING: *Not suitable*
COOKING TIME: *10 mins*   SERVES: *4*

Imperial (Metric)	American
1½ lb (675g) cooking apples	1½ pounds cooking apples
2 oz (50g) raisins	½ cup raisins
6 fl oz (175ml) red grape juice	¾ cup red grape juice
1 cinnamon stick	1 cinnamon stick
4 cloves	4 cloves
1 oz (25g) raw cane sugar	1½ tablespoons raw cane sugar

1 Peel, core and slice the apples and put them into a medium-sized pan with the raisins. Pour over the grape juice then add the cinnamon stick, cloves and sugar.
2 Bring the mixture to the boil then simmer, covered, for about 7 minutes, until the apples are soft but not reduced to a pulp.
3 Remove the cinnamon stick and cloves and serve warm or cold.

Banana and Sunflower Seed Fool

A light, creamy dessert with a wonderful fresh flavour. The fruity combination of bananas and grapes is delicious.

Bananas are a good source of carbohydrate and one banana supplies about half the day's requirements of vitamin B.

PREPARATION TIME: *10 mins*   FREEZING: *Not suitable*
COOKING TIME: *20 mins chill time*   SERVES: *4*

Imperial (Metric)	American
4 medium-sized ripe bananas	4 medium-sized ripe bananas
Rind and juice of 1 lemon	Rind and juice of 1 lemon
10 fl oz (300ml) Greek yoghurt	1¼ cups Greek yoghurt
2 tablespoons clear honey	2 tablespoons clear honey
2 tablespoons sunflower seeds	2 tablespoons sunflower seeds

To decorate
4 oz (100g/½ cup) seedless green grapes

1 Peel the bananas, chop them roughly and put them into a food processor.
2 Add the lemon rind and juice and blend to a purée.
3 Add the yoghurt and honey and blend again to mix well.
4 Fold in the sunflower seeds. Turn into wine glasses and chill for 20 minutes before serving, decorated with the grapes.

Caribbean Salad

Fresh fruits with lime and apple juice make a delicious, fresh-tasting dessert that's pretty enough for entertaining. Serve with fromage frais.

PREPARATION TIME: *15 mins* FREEZING: *Not suitable*
COOKING TIME: — SERVES: *4–6*

Imperial (Metric)
Rind and juice of ½ lime
5 fl oz (150ml) apple juice
1 fresh pineapple
4 oz (100g) fresh
  strawberries
8 oz (225g) white or red
  seedless grapes
2 medium-sized eating apples

American
Rind and juice of ½ lime
⅔ cup apple juice
1 fresh pineapple
1 cup fresh
  strawberries
1 cup white or red
  seedless grapes
2 medium-sized eating apples

1 Put the lime rind and juice into a large bowl with the apple juice.
2 Peel the pineapple, then dice the flesh roughly, discarding the core.
3 Hull and halve the strawberries and add to the bowl with the grapes and pineapple. Core and roughly chop the apples and add.
4 Toss everything together to ensure that all the fruit is coated with the juice. Serve immediately.

Lemon Whip with Plums

Plain yoghurt with low-fat fromage frais, honey and lemon juice for flavour makes a light, refreshing dessert. The plums add fibre and vitamin A.

PREPARATION TIME: *15 mins*   FREEZING: *Not suitable*
COOKING TIME: *15–20 mins chill time*   SERVES: *4*

Imperial (Metric)	American
5 fl oz (150ml) plain yoghurt	⅔ cup plain yoghurt
5 fl oz (150ml) low-fat fromage frais	⅔ cup low-fat fromage frais
2 egg whites	2 egg whites
2 teaspoons lemon juice	2 teaspoons lemon juice
1–2 tablespoons clear honey	1–2 tablespoons clear honey
4 large ripe plums	4 large ripe plums
Grated rind of 1 lemon	Grated rind of 1 lemon

1 Put the yoghurt and the fromage frais into a large mixing bowl. Stir to blend.
2 Using a clean whisk and bowl, beat the egg whites until stiff, then fold them into the yoghurt and fromage frais mixture with the lemon juice and honey.
3 Stone and roughly dice the plums. Fold into the mixture with the lemon rind.
4 Divide between 4 tall sundae glasses and chill for 15–20 minutes before serving.

Blackcurrant Pancakes

These pancakes store well in the freezer so may be prepared well in advance and used from frozen, if preferred. They will take about 1½ hours to thaw at room temperature.

Serve with fromage frais or plain yoghurt.

PREPARATION TIME: *20 mins*   FREEZING: *Suitable for the pancakes*
COOKING TIME: *25 mins*   MAKES: *6 pancakes*

Imperial (Metric)	American
For the pancakes	**For the pancakes**
4 oz (100g) wholewheat flour	1 cup wholewheat flour
1 egg	1 egg
10 fl oz (300ml) semi-skimmed milk	1¼ cups low-fat milk
Sunflower oil for frying	Sunflower oil for frying
For the filling	**For the filling**
7 oz (200g) can blackcurrants in natural juice	7-ounce can blackcurrants in natural juice
1 teaspoon arrowroot	1 teaspoon arrowroot

1 Prepare the batter: put the flour into a large mixing bowl. Crack the egg into the centre of the flour, then add half the milk. Beat with a wooden spoon, gradually drawing the flour into the liquid. Beat in the remaining milk until a smooth batter results. Set aside for 10 minutes.

2 To make the filling, strain the blackcurrants, reserving the juice.

3 Blend the arrowroot with the juice and pour into a small pan. Heat, stirring continuously, until boiling and slightly thickened. Stir in the blackcurrants and set aside.

4 Heat a small frying pan (skillet), then add 2 teaspoons of oil. Pour about 2 tablespoons of the batter into the hot pan.

5 Cook for 2–3 minutes until lightly golden underneath. Toss or turn the pancake and cook the other side for 1–2 minutes. Turn out on to a plate.
6 Continue until all the batter has been used up, stacking the pancakes as you go. Keep the pancakes warm, or cool and freeze at this stage, if required.
7 Spread each pancake with a little of the blackcurrant filling and roll up. Serve immediately.

Carrot Cake with Lemon Top

Healthy high-fibre carrot cake originated in Switzerland. The carrots add vitamin A and a particularly moist texture to this filling cake, which is delicious with a cup of tea. Ideal for children's lunch boxes too.

Although the cake takes about 50 minutes to cook, it is very quick and easy to mix using a food processor. You will need a 2 lb (1kg) loaf tin, about 9 × 5 × 4 in deep (23 × 13 × 10cm deep).

PREPARATION TIME: *20 mins*   FREEZING: *Suitable without the topping*
COOKING TIME: *50 mins*   MAKES: *a 2 lb (1kg) loaf*

Imperial (Metric)	American
2 medium carrots	2 medium carrots
2 eggs, beaten	2 eggs, beaten
3 oz (75g) raw cane sugar	½ cup raw cane sugar
4 fl oz (120ml) sunflower oil	½ cup sunflower oil
8 oz (225g) self-raising wholewheat flour	2 cups self-rising wholewheat flour
1 tablespoon semi-skimmed milk	1 tablespoon low-fat milk
1 teaspoon ground cinnamon	1 teaspoon ground cinnamon
½ teaspoon ground ginger	½ teaspoon ground ginger
2 oz (50g) dates, chopped	⅓ cup chopped dates
2 oz (50g) dried apricots, chopped	⅓ cup chopped dried apricots

For the optional topping

6 oz (175g) curd cheese	1½ cups pot cheese
Grated rind of ½ lemon	Grated rind of ½ lemon
1 oz (25g) raw cane sugar	1½ tablespoons raw cane sugar
2 teaspoons lemon juice	2 teaspoons lemon juice

1 Preheat the oven to gas mark 4, 350°F (180°C). Grease the loaf tin and line the base.
2 Cut each carrot into 3 pieces then chop them finely in a food processor using the metal blade. Add the eggs, sugar and oil and blend again just to combine.
3 Add the flour with the milk, cinnamon and ginger then process again, briefly, just to combine. Remove metal blade and fold in dates and apricots using a spoon.
4 Turn the mixture into the tin and level the surface, then bake in the centre of the oven for approximately 50 minutes, until a skewer inserted in the centre comes out clean.
5 Leave in the tin for 20 minutes then turn out on to a wire rack to cool.
6 Prepare the topping: turn the curd (pot) cheese into a mixing bowl. Beat in the lemon rind, sugar and lemon juice.
7 Spread evenly over the cake and swirl with a fork.

Apricot Slices

A quick-to-prepare cake that's particularly popular with children. There is plenty of fibre in these filling bars, which are much lower in fat than most cakes.

You will need a 7½ in (19cm) shallow, square cake tin.

PREPARATION TIME: *15 mins*   FREEZING: *Suitable*
COOKING TIME: *20 mins*   MAKES: *12 slices*

Imperial (Metric)	American
8 oz (225g) unsweetened muesli	2 cups unsweetened breakfast muesli
3 tablespoons wholewheat flour	3 tablespoons wholewheat flour
3 tablespoons sunflower oil	3 tablespoons sunflower oil
4 oz (100g) dried apricots	⅔ cup dried apricots
Grated rind and juice of ½ orange	Grated rind and juice of ½ orange
1 egg, beaten	1 egg, beaten

1 Preheat the oven to gas mark 4, 350°F (180°C). Lightly grease and base line the cake tin.
2 Mix together the muesli, flour and oil in a bowl. Snip the apricots into small pieces with scissors and add to the bowl with the orange rind and juice and the beaten egg.
3 Mix well to combine then turn the mixture into the prepared tin. Press down well.
4 Bake in the centre of the oven for about 20 minutes, until lightly golden.
5 Allow to cool completely. Turn out, remove the lining paper and cut into slices. Store in airtight container.

Creamy Layered Apricot Crunch

Apricot purée layered with low-fat fromage frais and
crunchy granola makes a quick and easy dessert that's
filling and fresh-tasting. You will find the recipe for
Granola on page 150.

PREPARATION TIME: *15 mins*   FREEZING: *Not suitable*
COOKING TIME: *30 mins chill time*   SERVES: *4*

Imperial (Metric)	American
14 oz (400g) can apricot slices in natural juice, drained	14-ounce can apricot slices in natural juice, drained
2 tablespoons clear honey	2 tablespoons clear honey
2 oz (50g) pecan nuts,	½ cup chopped pecan nuts
12 fl oz (350ml) low-fat fromage frais	1½ cups low-fat fromage frais
4–5 tablespoons granola	4–5 tablespoons granola
2 teaspoons raw cane sugar	2 teaspoons raw cane sugar

1 Put the apricot slices into a blender or food processor.
  Add 2 tablespoons of the juice and blend to a purée.
2 Stir the honey and nuts into the fromage frais.
3 Layer the granola, apricot purée and fromage frais
  mixture into 4 wine glasses, ending with a layer of
  fromage frais. Chill for 30 minutes.
4 Sprinkle with the sugar and serve immediately.

Creamy Rice and Redcurrant Swirl

This quickly made rice pudding is a delicious combination of redcurrants and Greek yoghurt. A creamy dessert which tastes luxurious, and provides some fibre and vitamin C.

PREPARATION TIME: *15 mins* FREEZING: *Not suitable*
COOKING TIME: *25 mins* SERVES: *4*

Imperial (Metric)
4 oz (100g) short-grain brown rice
5 fl oz (150ml) Greek yoghurt
4½ fl oz (135ml) semi-skimmed milk
2 tablespoons raw cane sugar
8 oz (225g) redcurrants
Grated rind of 1 lemon

American
1 cup short-grain brown rice
⅔ cup Greek yoghurt
⅔ cup low-fat milk
2 tablespoons raw cane sugar
2 cups redcurrants
Grated rind of 1 lemon

To decorate
Mint leaves

1 Cook the rice in a medium-sized pan of boiling water for 20–25 minutes, until just tender. Drain through a sieve (strainer) and rinse with plenty of cold water.
2 Mix together the yoghurt, milk and sugar.
3 Fold in the cooked rice with the redcurrants and the lemon rind, reserving a few redcurrants for decoration.
4 Spoon into 4 individual serving dishes. Refrigerate for 20 minutes or until well chilled.
5 Serve, garnished with the remaining redcurrants and the mint leaves.

Easy Peach Ice-Cream

This light, fruity ice-cream should be taken from the freezer and left at room temperature for 20–30 minutes before serving, so that the fresh flavour has a chance to develop. Serve with slices of fresh orange or peach for a delicious dessert that will be popular with everyone.

PREPARATION TIME: *20 mins*   FREEZING: *Suitable*
COOKING TIME: —   SERVES: *6*

Imperial (Metric)	American
2 large ripe peaches	2 large ripe peaches
4 fl oz (120ml) pure unsweetened orange juice	½ cup pure unsweetened orange juice
8 fl oz (250ml) low-fat plain yoghurt	1 cup low-fat plain yoghurt
Grated rind of 1 orange	Grated rind of 1 orange
1 egg white	1 egg white
1 oz (25g) raw cane sugar	1½ tablespoons raw cane sugar

To serve
Segments from 1 large
  orange or 1 large peach

1 Peel, stone and roughly chop the peaches. Put into a food processor with the orange juice. Blend to a purée then fold in the yoghurt.
2 Fold in the orange rind.
3 Pour into a shallow container and freeze for about 1½ hours, until the mixture becomes mushy round the edges. Turn into a bowl and beat with a wooden spoon.
4 Whisk the egg white in a clean bowl until stiff, then gradually whisk in the sugar to form a meringue.
5 Fold the meringue into the semi-frozen mixture and freeze until ready to serve.
6 Serve scoops of the ice-cream in sundae dishes, decorated with the orange or peach slices.

Drop Scones with Mango and Yoghurt

Quickly cooked drop scones are delicious served with sliced mango accompanied by plain yoghurt or fromage frais. Serve as a dessert or at tea time.

PREPARATION TIME: *15 mins*   FREEZING: *Suitable*
COOKING TIME: *15 mins*   MAKES: *about 14 drop scones*

Imperial (Metric)
4 oz (100g) self-raising wholewheat flour
1 egg
1 teaspoon sunflower oil plus a little extra for frying
7 fl oz (200ml) semi-skimmed milk

American
1 cup self-rising wholewheat flour
1 egg
1 teaspoon sunflower oil plus a little extra for frying
¾ cup low-fat milk

To serve
1 mango, peeled and sliced
Plain yoghurt or fromage frais

1 Put the flour into a mixing bowl. Make a well in the centre and break in the egg. Add the teaspoon of oil with the milk.
2 Gradually draw the dry ingredients into the liquid and beat with a wooden spoon to make a smooth, thick batter. Allow to stand for 5 minutes.
3 Lightly grease a large, heavy-based frying pan (skillet) with a little oil and place over a moderate heat, until hot.
4 Drop dessertspoonfuls of the mixture into the hot pan, keeping them well apart to allow for spreading. Cook for 2–3 minutes, until golden. Turn each scone over and continue to cook for a further 1–2 minutes, until golden.

5 Wrap the scones in a clean cloth to keep them warm while you cook the remainder, then serve them with the sliced mango, passing the yoghurt or fromage frais round separately.

Note: A delicious savoury drop scone may be made by stirring in 2 oz (50g/½ cup) strong grated Cheddar cheese to the batter after standing time. Serve warm with low-fat spread and sweet pickle or plain with a bowl of home made soup. The Sunshine Soup on page 20 would be ideal.

FURTHER READING

Brown, Sarah, *Sarah Brown's Healthy Living Cook Book*, Dorling Kindersley 1985
—— *Sarah Brown's Vegetarian Cook Book*, Dorling Kindersley 1987
The Cranks Recipe Book, Grafton Books 1982
Farrow, Joanna, *Quick & Easy Fish Cookery*, BBC Books 1992
Green, Henrietta and Marie Pierre Moine, *10 Minute Cuisine*, Octopus 1991
Hanford, Margaret, *The WI Book of Wholefood Cookery*, Merehurst 1985
Lindsay, Ann, *The Light Hearted Cook Book*, Grub Street 1991
Piper, Beverley, *Quick & Easy Healthy Cookery*, BBC Books 1992
—— *Super Juice*, Headline 1993

INDEX